14644477 1447259

Beyond Tests and Quizzes

Beyond Tests and Quizzes

*Creative Assessments
in the College Classroom*

Richard J. Mezeske
Barbara A. Mezeske

EDITORS

JOSSEY-BASS
A Wiley Imprint
www.josseybass.com

Published by Jossey-Bass
A Wiley Imprint
989 Market Street, San Francisco, CA 94103–1741   www.josseybass.com

Jossey-Bass books and products are available through most bookstores. To contact Jossey-Bass directly call our Customer Care Department within the U.S. at 800-956-7739, outside the U.S. at 317-572-3986, or fax 317-572-4002.

Jossey-Bass also publishes its books in a variety of electronic formats. Some content that appears in print may not be available in electronic books.

Library of Congress Cataloging-in-Publication Data
Beyond tests and quizzes : creative assessments in the college classroom / Richard J. Mezeske, Barbara A. Mezeske, editors. — 1st ed.
    p. cm.
Includes bibliographical references and index.
ISBN-13: 978-0-470-18083-9 (cloth)
1. College students—Rating of—Case studies.   2. Grading and marking (Students)—Case studies. 3. Creative teaching—Case studies. I. Mezeske, Richard J. II. Mezeske, Barbara A.
 LB2368.B49 2007
 378.1'66—dc22

                            2007023340

Printed in the United States of America
FIRST EDITION
HB Printing   10 9 8 7 6 5 4 3 2 1

To Janet L. Andersen, Ph.D., 1957–2005.

Teacher, mentor, friend.

Table of Contents

About the Authors

The Editors

Richard J. Mezeske is professor of teacher education and chair of the Department of Education at Hope College. His doctorate is from Michigan State University. His research interests include teacher learning and cognition, alternative assessment in literacy, and literature for children and adults. He has developed literacy courses taught for the college in Great Britain and has a long interest in building international relationships in teacher education. He is the 2004 recipient of the Janet L. Andersen Excellence in Teaching Award at Hope College. Richard is the coeditor of and a contributing author to *Finding Our Way: Teacher Education Reform in the Liberal Arts Setting* (Peter Lang, 2004).

Barbara A. Mezeske is associate professor in the English department at Hope College where she is the director of Freshmen Composition, director of the Faculty Mentoring program, and staff member of the Teaching Enhancement Workshop for new faculty. She has written widely on assessment and pedagogy. She received the Janet L. Andersen Excellence in Teaching Award at Hope College in 1998. Barbara is the coeditor of *Finding Our Way: Teacher Education Reform in the Liberal Arts Setting* (Peter Lang, 2004).

The Contributors

Susan Cherup, professor, holds the Arnold and Esther Sonneveldt endowed chair in education at Hope College. She was invited to serve on the team that wrote the National Educational Technology Standards for Teachers and is president of the Special Education Technology, Special Interest Group of the International Society for Technology in Education. Her teaching areas include special education, technology, and Indian studies. Susan was awarded the

Janet L. Andersen Excellence in Teaching Award at Hope College in 1999.

Mary J. DeYoung teaches mathematics to pre-service elementary teachers at Hope College. Her classroom is renowned for the box of unlimited mathematical "stuff" that she uses regularly with her college students. She also enjoys leading workshops for teachers in area schools; problem solving and active learning for students of all ages are her particular interests. Mary received her B.A. in mathematics at Hope College and her M.A. in mathematics education at Western Michigan University.

Lee Forester is associate professor of German in the Department of Modern and Classical Languages at Hope College. He received his Ph.D. in Germanic linguistics from the University of California–Berkeley. His current research focuses on the use of computers in foreign language instruction. Lee is the author of *Umlaut Phenomena in Early German Discourse* (Peter Lang, 1999) and is coeditor of *Auf geht's! Beginning German Language and Culture* (2005) and *Weiter geht's! Intermediate German Language and Culture* (2007).

Elizabeth Gayton received her Ph.D. from Southampton University, United Kingdom, in neuroscience. After some years teaching in secondary schools in the United Kingdom, she became a lecturer in biology at Liverpool Hope University, eventually being named head of the biology program and then head of the School of Science and Social Science. Her passion for student learning led to her appointment as associate dean for learning and teaching at Liverpool Hope, where she is currently the dean of education. Elizabeth leads programs in both undergraduate and postgraduate teacher education and subjects allied to education.

Janis M. Gibbs is associate professor and chair of the Department of History at Hope College. She holds degrees from the College of William and Mary (B.A.), the University of Chicago (J.D.), and the University of Virginia (M.A. and Ph.D.). Her research focuses on religion, society, and identity in early modern Germany, especially the city of Cologne. Janis's teaching interests include medieval and early modern Europe, the Middle East, and civil liberties law in the United States.

Rhoda Janzen teaches American literature, grammar, and poetry at Hope College. A faculty member since 2000, she has a Ph.D. and an M.A. in American literature from UCLA and an M.A. in creative writing from the University of Florida. Her first book of poetry, *Babel's Stair*, will be published in 2007 by Word Press. Rhoda is currently writing a textbook called *Grammar in Action*.

Michael Misovich is an associate professor of engineering at Hope College. He has also served on the faculty of Rose-Hulman Institute of Technology and Villanova University, where he was awarded the Farrell Memorial Award for service to the College of Engineering. Michael's research area is physical property prediction for chemical engineering, and he also has been active in engineering education and assessment.

Richard Ray is coordinator of the athletic training program and professor and chair of the Department of Kinesiology at Hope College. His undergraduate degree is from the University of Michigan; his master's in athletic training and a doctorate in educational leadership are from Western Michigan University. He serves on the editorial board of the *Journal of Athletic Training* and is the former editor-in-chief of *Athletic Therapy Today.* He has a wide range of scholarly interests and has received 18 grants to support his work. He is the author or coauthor of three books published by Human Kinetics Publishing, *Management Strategies in Athletic Training* (now in its third edition, 2005), *Counseling in Sports Medicine* (1999), and *Case Studies in Athletic Training Administration* (1995). Richard has authored more than

40 articles in scientific publications and presented papers at a similar number of local, regional, national, and international conferences and symposia. He has served in a variety of appointed and elected positions in the National Athletic Trainers' Association and other related organizations. In 2000, Richard received the Janet L. Andersen Excellence in Teaching Award from Hope College.

Carla Reyes is assistant professor in the Counseling Psychology Doctoral Program in the Department of Educational Psychology at the University of Utah. She received her B.A. from the University of Kansas and her Ph.D. in counseling/clinical/school psychology from the University of California–Santa Barbara. Her research and clinical interests include examining resiliency in abused children, prevention and intervention for at-risk children, play therapy, and multicultural counseling. Carla is a licensed clinical psychologist and maintains an active private practice.

David B. Schock is a filmmaker who earned his doctorate studying with the late Russell Amos Kirk. His degree is in creative writing and literary criticism. He also holds a master's degree in journalism and a bachelor's degree in religion. One of his recent films, *Who Killed Janet Chandler?*, resulted in the fielding of an investigative team. The result of the team, after two years of nonstop work, was the arrest of those accused of Miss Chandler's murder. In addition to unsolved homicides, David studies and documents the Ku Klux Klan. He's also a jazz trumpet player.

Thomas Smith is the Dr. Leon A. Bosch '29 Professor of Management at Hope College. He received his Ph.D. from the University of Michigan in 1994. His areas of research interest are operations strategy and Christian perspectives on management and teaching. He has published articles in a variety of journals including *Journal of Operations Management, International Journal of Produc-*

tion Research, Journal of Biblical Integration in Business, Christian Higher Education, and *Christian Business Academy Review.* In addition to life in academia, Tom spent five years in various manufacturing management positions with Data General Corporation, has consulted with several local businesses, and was the Women's Golf Coach at Hope from 2000–2005.

Elizabeth A. Trembley is a creative writing instructor in both nonfiction and fiction and administers two programs for first-year students struggling to succeed academically. She has presented nationally on the use of the Herrmann Brain Dominance Instrument™ in educational settings and has offered training on its use in developing creativity for college administrators and in the business world. In addition to short stories, essays, and articles, she has published a book on the fiction of Michael Crichton and coedited a volume on the adaptation of detective fiction for film. Elizabeth received her B.A. from Hope College and her M.A. and Ph.D. from the University of Chicago.

Scott VanderStoep is associate professor of psychology, chair of the Department of Psychology, and director of academic assessment at Hope College. He has taught courses in introductory, developmental, and cognitive psychology for 14 years. He has a Ph.D. in education and psychology from the University of Michigan. Scott is the author (with Paul Pintrich) of *Learning to Learn: The Skill and Will of College Success* (Prentice-Hall, 2002) and the editor of *Science and the Soul: Christian Faith and Psychological Research* (University Press of America, 2003).

Roger Veldman is associate professor of engineering at Hope College. He joined the faculty in 1998 after working in engineering and product development at Herman Miller Inc. and Donnelly Corporation (now Magna Donnelly). Roger's research area is mechanical response of structures subject to explosions, and he also holds more than 25 patents for the design of mirrors and other automotive components.

Kathy Winnett-Murray received a B.S. in biological sciences from the University of California–Irvine (1976), an M.S. in biology from California State University–Northridge (1979), and a Ph.D. in zoology from the University of Florida (1986). She is professor of biology at Hope College where she teaches introductory biology, animal behavior, zoology, and ecology courses for nonscience majors. Her research interests include behavioral ecology of birds and the ecology of invasive species. She participates in a wide variety of science outreach (K–12) programs. Kathy was the recipient of the College Teacher of the Year Award given by the Michigan Science Teacher's Association (1997–1998), and she received the Janet L. Andersen Excellence in Teaching Award from Hope College in 2006.

Acknowledgments

One might imagine a battle of wits whenever 14 academics sit down together to consider the subject of assessment. One faction may take on a strident tone and declare that no one will tell them how to teach. Another group might be concerned about answering to the so-called higher powers of local, state, and national governments. We've encountered neither of these attitudes in working with our 14 colleagues from Hope College who have developed a range of tools for assessing student learning in their classrooms. We are grateful to them for their willingness to share their ideas, for their open-minded approach to the topic of assessment, and for their dedication to and focus on student learning. As you read these chapters, keep in mind the range of backgrounds and areas of expertise that influence the work of these colleagues.

The editors are also grateful to Michael Jipping, professor of computer science at Hope College, for his unstinting assistance with technical matters. These include, especially, preparing graphics for publication.

Finally, we acknowledge the climate for good teaching and ongoing assessment that has been nurtured at Hope College by a supportive administration, creative faculty, hardworking departmental assessment teams, and nationally accredited programs in nursing, dance, teacher education, chemistry, athletic training, social work, art, music, theatre, and engineering.

To the critics of mandated assessments, we merely say, read on!

Richard J. Mezeske
Barbara A. Mezeske
Hope College
January 2007

Introduction: Why These Assessment Opportunities Make Sense in a World Where Assessment of Factual Knowledge Has Taken Hold

Elizabeth Gayton

What might students in higher education fear most? The judgments of their professors. These judgments may be the most important things that happen to them. However, at the end of the day, it is what students can show they have learned, at a given time and in a given format, that counts. In addition, there is no doubt that assessment is very powerful in defining what students regard as important, how they spend their time, and how they come to see themselves as students and graduates (Brown, Bull, & Pendlebury, 1997). Understanding the power of good assessment is of paramount importance to both student and tutor.

The word *assessment* actually derives from an idea important to all current-day educators, that of *sitting down beside or together* (from the Latin *ad* and *sidere*). Three hundred years ago, an assessor was *one who sits beside* or *who shares another's position.* In those days, assessment focused almost exclusively on determining the worth or value of something in monetary terms, but underlying those uses was the idea of expert judgment made on the basis of careful observation (Loacker, Cromwell, & O'Brien, 1986). Literally *sitting down beside* the increasing number of students in a modern classroom is an obvious impossibility for faculty in higher education today, but the support and guidance implicit in this concept is developed by good teachers everywhere. What really matters is not so much what teachers provide but what learners achieve.

The United Kingdom Quality Assurance Agency for Higher Education (QAA) defines assessment as "any processes that appraise an individual's knowledge, understanding, abilities or skills" (QAA, 2006, p. 4). A deeper and much more valuable appreciation of assessment is that it is "the systematic collection, review, and use of information about educational programs . . . for the purpose of improving student learning and development" (Palomba & Banta, 1999, p. 4). This definition implies correctly that assessment can serve many purposes. Formative assessment should provide students with feedback so they can judge both the progress of their learning and the efficacy of their study methods. Summative assessment provides information on student achievement at the end of a particular unit of study. This can be the basis of selection for subsequent courses and/or future employment. Whether, of course, this is a predictor of future performance is debatable (Elton & Johnston, 2002). Faculty also need knowledge about student performance to modify and improve their teaching and assessment strategies. External bodies use the outcome of assessments to assure public accountability. And like it or not, assessment is often the driving force that pushes a student toward serious study.

The relative importance of these objectives depends on the interests of the parties concerned. Students are increasingly being seen (and are seeing themselves) as customers and are making growing demands on educational institutions to deliver a high-quality product at a reasonable cost. Managers in higher education, on one hand, advocate early assessment as a retention tool and, on the other, use assessment results as a means of measuring the success in meeting retention targets. Employers, professional bodies, funding bodies, government, and the media all claim an interest in the assessment process. Of all the activities involved in being a teacher in higher education, few are more important than assessment of students.

"Students can with difficulty escape from the effects of poor teaching . . . they cannot (by definition if they wish to graduate) escape from the effects of poor assessment" (Boud, 1995, p. 35). Assessment is unavoidable for both students and faculty. Furthermore, students and faculty spend a large portion of their time either performing or evaluating assessments. An analysis from Robert Gordon University in Scotland showed that students in computing courses spent 96 hours per semester on in-course assessment alone, much of which was crammed into the second half of the semester (Brown, 2003). A quick calculation for one department at my own university, Liverpool Hope, showed that education students produced 15,362 pieces of coursework per year. This was marked by about 50 faculty. At a conservative estimate of 20 minutes per assignment, this means that each faculty member spent 100 hours grading even before being involved in second marking and moderation. Second marking involves a predetermined sample of assignments, approximately 20% of the total, which are read by a second faculty member in an effort to ensure, as far as possible, objectivity. So it is imperative that any activity involving so much time for both students and faculty must be effective, fit for purpose, worthwhile, and efficient.

Assessment plays a significant role in the learning experience of students. Not only does it determine their progression through their program of study, but it also allows them to demonstrate that they have met the learning outcomes and the conditions recognized by external qualifications. More significantly, perhaps, good assessment can be used by students as part of their learning strategies as well as allowing them to assess the development of their study skills and act as motivators. There is no doubt that how students are assessed has a profound effect on what they learn and on the ways in which they learn (Brown, Race, & Smith, 1996). Students bring their own motivations and preferred approaches to their learning. Institutional culture, course design, and faculty attitudes can have a profound influence on the strategies adopted by students. Much has been written about deep and surface approaches to learning

(Gibbs, 1981; Marton & Säljö, 1997; Ramsden, 1997) as well as styles of learning (Honey & Mumford, 1992; Kolb, 1984). While it could be argued that teaching strategies and assignment tasks should be designed for students dependent on their learning styles, this is often neither practical nor desirable. However, an understanding of the issues surrounding styles of learning will ensure that faculty take this into account when designing the curriculum to maximize support of learning for all students, not just some.

The focus of faculty on assessment undoubtedly varies with the evolution of their teaching abilities. A model by Peter Kugel (1993) describes the early stages in this process as one where teachers focus on themselves and their subject. At a later stage there is a realization that the students actually have a significant role in the learning process, closely followed by an understanding of the need for this to be an active role and eventually that their students should become autonomous learners. Somewhere along this continuum the emphasis shifts from teaching to learning, and this is usually accompanied by an appreciation of the role of assessment in achieving this shift. Good assessment has a clear purpose and achievable criteria understood by both faculty and student. It is valid and feasible, meeting the purpose for which it was designed within the context of numbers of students and available resources. It is fully integrated into the unit of study relating directly to the theoretical and practical components of the course. Significantly, good assessment includes good feedback delivered in a timely, supportive, and accurate manner that motivates students to develop their understanding of the subject and enhance their study practice.

Ramsden (1992) describes three models of teaching: teaching as telling, teaching as organizing student activity, and teaching as making learning possible. Those who are proficient in this third way are those who are most likely to strive to provide a learning environment that takes into account models of student learning. The chapters in this book are written by faculty who are truly reflective practitioners and who regard teaching as a means to an end, the end being their students' learning. Although the focus of their writing is on assessment, it is evident that this assessment is integrated into the whole student learning experience. The authors hail from a range of disciplines, and each provides a snapshot of how specific assignment tasks fit seamlessly into their programs. However, they all have one thing in common. The assessments described all contribute to the creation of an environment conducive to learning, which attempts to recognize both the educational and cultural background of the students.

The academic underpinning of assessment of students in higher education has been widely researched and documented. Many faculty members are so involved with the business of balancing the demands of teaching, research, and administration, as well as the pastoral support of their students, that addressing the theory and philosophy of assessment design and implementation is often approached as an afterthought. The value of a book like this is that it is written by colleagues who are also trying to balance those demands but have taken the opportunity to think about their students, curricula, and assignments and can pass on easily digestible advice and ideas. It is not a book written predominantly by Hope College faculty for Hope College faculty. Without a doubt, I recommend this as a book for higher education faculty anywhere in the world to consider. Each chapter can be taken in isolation. Don't allow yourself to be limited by the not-my-subject approach. Many of the examples are not subject specific, and with a little imagination, all are transferable. For example, the principles of the engineering design project described in Chapter 10 could be translated into programs on art or information technology. Teacher educators may well resonate with the clinical proficiency transcript in Chapter 11.

The authors have approached assessment in full recognition of the diversity of their students' educational and cultural experiences. They believe passionately that assessment should promote active learning and is most effective when firmly placed in the context of the real world. They have grappled with issues of plagiarism, surface learning, and student responsibility and autonomy. They know that students themselves need to have clearly articulated and transparent guidelines and criteria. Equally important, they are aware that, as professional educators, they can use student performance to influence the evolution of programs of study and the nature of assessment tasks. The narratives indicate that they are not working in isolation but in teams with (often) like-minded colleagues. The following highlights provide a taste of some of the material covered; it is not exhaustive nor is it intended to diminish any chapter or author not mentioned.

Objective exams are becoming increasingly popular as a method of assessment that minimizes issues associated with plagiarism. The main criticism of such an assessment is that it tests recall and does not allow for constructive feedback. Thomas Smith (Chapter 6) describes how he uses such exams as a "significant learning opportunity" for both students and instructors. The feasibility of translating his strategy directly into a different context will depend on a number of factors, not least the number of students and time available. That said, it may be that some of the principles can be used. For example, although the individual review sessions are undoubtedly valuable, if they are not feasible then students may still be able to benefit from cheat sheets, review sessions, access to previous exam papers, and practice answers, all of which have a sound rationale.

Recognizing that students come to class with different strengths and weaknesses, Barbara A. Mezeske (Chapter 3) empowers her students to take control of their learning by offering them a choice of assessment tasks. Her use of learning logs not only gives insight into the students' views of the course and its assessment but encourages students to engage with the all important concept of meta-learning

(Biggs, 1985). In other words, they have the chance to improve their ability to understand what and (perhaps more significantly) how they are learning and plan accordingly. Allowing students to negotiate or choose their assessment task offers opportunities for students to develop personal engagement and autonomy and also addresses issues relating to individualized learning and preferred learning styles. Building on the premise that students learn by doing, David B. Schock (Chapter 14) has designed his curricula so that what students learn reflects and builds on their individual interests and strengths. He describes courses with an element of "outside learning" in which students strive to meet institutional standards as well as the expectations of an outside agency and in doing so find that "learning becomes alive."

Creative and imaginative approaches to supporting learning are evident in most chapters, none more so than Janis M. Gibbs's History Workshop (Chapter 4) and Rhoda Janzen's "Verbing the Noun" (Chapter 12). Gibbs has devised pseudo-documentary evidence relating to the death of the Witch of the East from *The Wizard of Oz*. These mirror the genuine historical artifacts, and their interpretation allows students from varied backgrounds to engage, on equal footing, with the development of the skills of an academic historian. Janzen challenges cultural assumptions about grammar in a way that not only addresses the yawn factor but also empowers students to become personally accountable for the errors of their own writing.

There is no doubt that the role and importance of assessment in the enhancement of student learning is an issue for higher education worldwide, and faculty interested in curriculum planning may gain inspiration from the examples provided in this book. Of course, there may well be tensions between the ideas put forward here and the practicalities of particular circumstances. However, a constructively critical approach and a willingness to be open and imaginative will reap dividends in terms of both student and faculty learning. Enjoy!

References

Biggs, J. B. (1985). The role of meta-learning in study processes. *British Journal of Educational Psychology, 55,* 185–212.

Boud, D. (1995). Assessment and learning: Contradictory or complementary. In P. Knight (Ed.), *Assessment for learning in higher education* (pp. 35–38). London, UK: Kogan Page.

Brown, D. (2003). Assessment: Lightening the load. In W. Hornby, *Strategies for streamlining assessment.* Retrieved May 2, 2007, from http://ssrn.com/abstract=410263

Brown, G., Bull, J., & Pendlebury, M. (1997). *Assessing student learning in higher education.* London, UK: Routledge.

Brown, S., Race, P., & Smith, B. (1996). *500 tips on assessment.* London, UK: Kogan Page.

Elton, L., & Johnston, B. (2002). *Assessment in universities: A critical review of research.* Retrieved May 2, 2007, from www.heacademy.ac.uk/resources.asp?process=full_recor d&section=generic&id=13

Gibbs, G. (1981). *Teaching students to learn: A student-centered approach.* Milton Keynes, UK: Open University Press.

Honey, P., & Mumford, A. (1992). *The manual of learning styles.* Maidenhead, UK: Peter Honey.

Kolb, D. A. (1984). *Experiential learning: Experience as a source of learning and development.* Upper Saddle River, NJ: Prentice Hall.

Kugel, P. (1993). How professors develop as teachers. *Studies in Health Education, 18*(3), 315–328.

Loacker, G., Cromwell, C., & O'Brien, K. (1986). Assessment in higher education: To serve the learner. In C. Adelman (Ed.), *Assessment in American higher education: Issues and contexts* (pp. 47–62). Washington, DC: U.S. Department of Education.

Marton, F., & Säljö, R. (1997). Approaches to learning. In F. Marton, D. J. Hounsell, & N. J. Entwistle (Eds.), *The experience of learning: Implications for teaching and studying in higher education* (2nd ed., pp. 39–58). Edinburgh, Scotland: Scottish Academic Press.

Palomba, C. A., & Banta, T. W. (1999). *Assessment essentials: Planning, implementing, and improving assessment in higher education.* San Francisco, CA: Jossey-Bass.

Quality Assurance Agency. (2006). *Code of practice for the assurance of academic quality and standards in higher education: Section 6: Assessment of students.* Retrieved May 2, 2007, from www.qaa.ac.uk/academicinfrastructure/code OfPractice/section6/COP_AOS.pdf

Ramsden, P. (1992). *Learning to teach in higher education.* London, UK: Routledge.

Ramsden, P. (1997). The context of learning in academic departments. In F. Marton, D. J. Hounsell, & N. J. Entwistle (Eds.), *The experience of learning: Implications for teaching and studying in higher education* (2nd ed., pp. 198–216). Edinburgh, Scotland: Scottish Academic Press.

1

Why Creative Assessment?

Richard J. Mezeske, Barbara A. Mezeske

It should be obvious to even the casual observer that an intensive focus on external assessment is driving educational reform around the world. Americans have the No Child Left Behind legislation, while the British have a version called Every Child Matters. Each set of laws has been imposed on schools and teachers by government bodies through a political process. None of the authors in this book intend to focus on the political debate regarding these laws; standardized assessment/evaluation is now a fact of life. Accountability and responsibility of the academic community to all learners is something we accept. However, because the drive toward external assessment speaks almost exclusively in terms of standardized testing, we need to be reminded of the internal purposes of assessment—measuring learning for both student and teacher so instruction can be adjusted and improved, not to satisfy an outsider with relatively uninformative statistics on how many students answered C on a multiple choice test. Our intent in this book is to present a more nuanced use of assessment in the contexts of everyday college classrooms and disciplines with a varied range of learners.

In his academic mystery novel, *The Missing Professor* (2006), Thomas B. Jones discusses the role(s) for assessment at the fictional Higher State University where professors sound suspiciously like people we know who hear the word assessment and hastily excuse themselves from the room. We provide his comments here as examples of what we do not mean by assessment:

First, assessment is time taken away from teaching and research, not to mention advising students. . . . Second, we are simply attempting to satisfy external agents and bureaucratic legislative idiots with a flurry of inapplicable, inconsequential mass testing and bogus statistical conclusions. . . . Third, assessment at this university and elsewhere generally demonstrates no trust in our skills and learning as professors. It's insulting. Fourth, you ask a bunch of students into a mass test that has no relationship to their classes here at Higher State and I guarantee you they won't participate . . . (pp. 2–3)

In Jones's fictional state university, assessment makes people shudder. But unlike the teachers at Higher State, many of us teach in vibrant academic communities that are fostering thoughtful deliberations about assessment, its meanings, and its uses in rigorous academic programs. Both formally and informally, faculty at institutions of higher learning all over the country are engaged in a variety of initiatives, both individual and collaborative, which strive to better serve student learning and rigorous teaching.

As noted earlier, it is not our intention in this volume to provide a venue for assessment bashing within the current national and international debates about accountability, funding, responses to outside stakeholders, and issues of control. Nor do we intend to use endless pages to defend academic freedom versus the emerging new attitudes about assessment. Rather, the authors of these chapters have a particular sense of the value creative assessment can and should play in their teaching and in student learning. We believe assessment is a necessary tool for refining the work of teaching and learning; otherwise, some of us might do nothing to change the status quo. Without assessment as experience, we might resist structures related to useful, day-to-day assessment.

These chapters are focused on the very real efforts of college classroom instructors to meaningfully measure what they are teaching and what their students are learning. While these faculty efforts are not always affirmed by statistical T-scores and correlations, they are affirmed in other ways: higher levels of student engagement, measurable increases in direct student participation in courses, and improved collaboration between and among students. Each of these examples can and does lead to a deeper understanding of content and, therefore, may aid and foster improved performance on mandated tests. In the end, these authors also want their students to know and use content knowledge. Like Richard Feynman (see below) we also want students to deeply understand the ramifications of factual knowledge.

Assessment Defined

It should be obvious that assessment can be defined in many ways depending on its uses and the contexts in which it is applied. For our purposes, assessment is defined in a straightforward manner. We cite several variations on a theme below:

- "Assessment is the gathering of information about learners in order to make temporary decisions about instruction" (Harris & Hodges, 1995, p. 12).
- "Assessment is the systematic collection, review, and use of information about educational programs undertaken for the purpose of improving student learning and development" (Palomba & Banta, 1999, p. 4).
- "Classroom assessment is an approach designed to help teachers find out what students are learning in the classroom and how well they are learning it. This approach is learner centered, teacher directed, mutually beneficial, context specific, ongoing, and firmly rooted in good practice" (Angelo & Cross, 1993, p. 4). "The type of assessment most likely to improve teaching and learning is that conducted by faculty to answer questions they themselves have formulated in response to issues or problems in their own teaching" (p. 9).

Thus, as the reader can clearly see, we strive to lay out ways in which college teachers can affect learning in their own classrooms through a variety of assessment tools that respond to the real needs of learners, and not just at the end of a semester or term. The approaches suggested in this book focus on learning, on what students can do as a result of learning, and on how teachers can observe what students do. Furthermore, thinking of assessment in this way can allow teachers to change instruction midcourse and then shape and inform subsequent instruction to produce better learning.

So while some might see assessment as a measure to prove something to an external observer (or a state or legislature), we see assessment as an integral and essential part of what educators do: We measure the effects of our instruction. Readers of these chapters will quickly discern the focus of each author: improved teaching and learning of content. The authors of these chapters have found ways to monitor student learning that hold students accountable for context, application, and flexible habits of mind. We invite readers of this book to consider the applications described here and to tweak them, to adapt them, and to use them creatively for the support of learning that goes well beyond rote recall and memorizing facts. Facts do not solve problems in the real world. Rather it is how these facts are interpreted, applied, and used that makes all the difference.

Why Creative Assessment?

So why bother to focus on creative forms of assessment instead of the customary objective test that is easily graded with a Scantron machine? Is there anything wrong with the conventional test, the essay, or the research paper? Of course not. In fact, many teachers make wonderfully inventive and effective use of standard assessment tools. When we speak of *creative* assessment in this book, we are talking about assessments that spin, twist, and reform what might be a standard kind of assessment in an ordinary classroom.

The authors of this work believe that we are obligated to make sure that our students not only know the *facts* but know the material in *meaningful* ways. That means learners must flexibly and creatively use that factual content to solve real-world problems and to develop habits of mind for dealing with life so they are not smacked down at failure; they merely try another approach, gather more or other data, and effectively change their response. Recitation of facts, without conscious and meaningful applications to the real world in which we all live, gives learning little meaning and makes it impractical at best.

The chapters included here represent a cross section of the possibilities available to classroom teachers who are willing to step out of their comfort zones and who ask how teaching affects learning. When that barrier is crossed, options become available, substance can be addressed, and outside stakeholders will still have the evidence they need to support schools and teachers. There is no shortage of reports in the media of business leaders who decry the inability of workers to solve problems in the workplace and to collaborate with others to find solutions to problems for real people. In his book *Surely You're Joking, Mr. Feynman: Adventures of a Curious Character* (1985), physicist Richard P. Feynman describes his encounter with a group of brilliant Brazilian physics students working with reflection and polarized light. They captured his every word in copious notes, they could recite the details of his lectures, they knew the facts and could recall lengthy definitions and formulae. In the end, however, what they could not do was to explain in plain language what they learned and to what uses it could be put. Feynman reported,

> After a lot of investigation, I finally figured out that the students had memorized everything, but they didn't know what anything meant. When they heard "light was reflected from a medium inside an index," they didn't know it meant in a material *such as water.* They didn't know that the "direction of light" is the

direction in which you *see* something when you're looking at it, and so on. Everything was entirely memorized, yet nothing had been translated into meaningful words. (pp. 212–213)

Feynman noticed what the authors of this volume also notice. Memorization is not enough; knowledge must end up in practice and doing. And that may well mean moving outside of accepted or normal practice. Feynman was appalled with the shallowness of his students' learning and their inability to make sense of newly acquired factual storehouses. We suggest that current college instructors should likewise not settle for factual knowledge by itself.

How Should Assessment Serve Students and Teachers for Instructional Purposes?

So how should college teachers use these examples of creative assessment? They should consider them to be starting points and the beginning of an internal discussion on what matters most in the courses they teach. What components of each course count the most for solving a range of problems in this discipline? If facts are important, and they usually are, how can they be used to support a flexible approach to thinking, solving, considering options, gathering, and interpreting evidence? What are the facts not telling us? We believe that creative assessments, like the ones in this book, should be used alongside a range of assessments, even including objective tests and standardized tools, to build a multifaceted, agile thinking citizenry who do more than *do what they're told.*

References

Angelo, T. A., & Cross, K. P. (1993). *Classroom assessment techniques: A handbook for college teachers* (2nd ed.). San Francisco, CA: Jossey-Bass.

Feynman, R. P. (1985). *Surely you're joking, Mr. Feynman: Adventures of a curious character.* New York, NY: W. W. Norton.

Harris, T. L., & Hodges, R. E. (Eds.). (1995). *The literacy dictionary: The vocabulary of reading and writing.* Newark, DE: International Reading Association.

Jones, T. B. (2006). *The missing professor: An academic mystery.* Sterling, VA: Stylus.

Palomba, C. A., & Banta, T. W. (1999). *Assessment essentials: Planning, implementing, and improving assessment in higher education.* San Francisco, CA: Jossey-Bass.

2

Concept Mapping: Assessing Pre-Service Teachers' Understanding and Knowledge

Richard J. Mezeske

For years I have been acutely aware that traditional objective and essay exams were limited in what they told me about the knowledge base and performance of teacher candidates in my courses. To be sure, I had a sense of what factual material they were able to explain on these exams. On the other hand, these exams were not always good tools to help me or my students clarify how a teacher's knowledge could inform his or her actions in the classroom. Nor could they completely explain what links were being made by these aspiring teachers between theory and practice. There needed to be more integration of factual knowledge with the realities of classroom life, the very real problems involved in teaching content subjects, and the diversity of learner populations in P–12 classrooms. Teacher candidates needed extensive opportunities for reflection and critical analysis of content, methodology, materials, student populations, the theory-practice continuum, and research in the field.

Some of these opportunities for reflection are directly connected to field experiences tied to each departmental course. Some are tied directly to performances and presentations in college classrooms. Yet professors in my program wanted still more opportunities for critical analysis of the pre-service teachers' knowledge base, and of how that knowledge was integrated with the students' field observations, with their own extensive experience as school learners, and with their expectations about the sort of teachers they would become.

With this agenda in mind, I attended a lengthy workshop at the 1992 Michigan Reading Association annual conference. The workshop was about concept mapping as a means for encouraging pre-service teachers to graphically represent what they know and understand about the superordinate, coordinate, and subordinate components of education courses. Cathleen Rafferty, leader of the workshop, cited work done by many others (Rafferty & Fleschner, 1993) to demonstrate the efficacy of mapping. Concept maps, primarily in hierarchical or linear format, require candidates to link major ideas and concepts of course content and to justify the relationships between them. The maps described in this workshop were not entirely linear nor were they simple flow charts; nevertheless, they did not tend to vary from the superordinate, coordinate, and subordinate hierarchical arrangement and model. In a sense they were metaphors within a framework for the ways in which individuals understood and viewed a particular concept or set of concepts.

The next semester I experimented with concept mapping as a final exam. I was not entirely sure what I wanted, let alone what students would produce in the end. Some students were horrified at what I was asking them to do—they had always been successful on objective exams and wanted to stay in their comfort zones. Others were wary but also interested in trying something new. Ultimately, my students rose to the occasion and were relieved to try something other than an objective or essay final exam. Predictably, results were scattered. Some students immediately focused on current substantive course content and built meaningful connections to teaching practice. Some built connections with previous coursework in educational psychology. Still others struggled to understand what it meant to make logical connections and to justify these connections. Some students remained at a superficial level of content recall, yet others saw the possibilities for expressing their unique points of view on these links.

Figure 2.1 Peanut Store Concept Map

In the end, I was surprised and pleased by what pre-service teachers knew about the course content and by how they viewed the interrelationships among concepts, content, research, and day-to-day teaching practice. Almost immediately, however, students in these courses started asking permission to embellish their maps, to select themes and metaphors, and to vary the map from the hierarchical or linear format. They wanted to move from simple flow charts and graphics to more personal representations of knowledge. After all, they had been made acutely aware that not all learners see the world in the same way—some perspectives are more global and less structured. I was wary, but the risk has proven to be worth it. The metaphors students chose were often personal, connected to their everyday interests, work lives, or to their subject areas, but each was always used a means for helping others understand what

Figure 2.2 Orchestra Concept Map

the creator knew and understood. For example, one student chose the metaphor of a local peanut store where she worked as a clerk (see Figure 2.1). After drawing a simple outline of the store interior, she inserted actual wrappers from a wide range of candies sold in the store to represent components of literacy learning that she believed were important and worth noting: Swedish Fish came to stand for cultural and ethnic diversity, other candies represented the role of technology, and so on. Lines drawn on the floor represent connections between concepts. Notice on this map the intricate ways in which the creator used the everyday to parallel the academic and social aspects of learning.

In Figure 2.2, a secondary music education major mapped out the components and links he deemed important for an orchestra classroom supported by literacy principles. The conductor, in this case a teacher, leads a variety of players not only to encourage fine musicianship but also to attend to myriad factors that come into play in any content subject classroom: parents, community, self-esteem and confidence

Figure 2.3 Paris Metro Concept Map

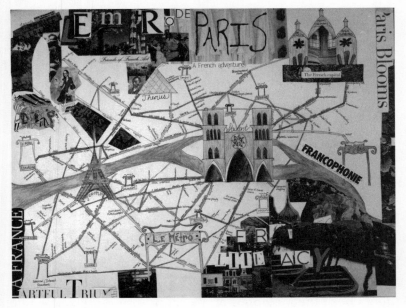

issues, as well as safety in the music classroom. These were components that not only reflected the mapmaker's sense of what it means to be literate in a music classroom but also a representation of other educational concepts he had learned from previous courses.

Each semester my students produce a stunning array of graphic representations about the connections between their content subject majors and minors and teaching and learning. Faculty from these major and minor subject departments frequently tour these maps at the end of the semester—they are equally amazed at the work of their students.

It is important to understand what these students wanted when they asked permission to include metaphors. They wanted to personalize what they knew and understood and link that understanding to the prior knowledge they brought to the course. One secondary level dance/French

Figure 2.4 Refrigerator Concept Map

major, for example, centered her entire map around the image of the Paris subway system, the Metro. The beauty of this metaphor (see Figure 2.3) was the natural links and connections it provided to the map builder. She used the tracks and stations and Paris landmarks to provide her graphic representation of what she understood about learning French, general literacy, and the many factors that affect learning both within school and outside it, such as social conflict, drugs, media, educational theories, and French culture. The subway routes are the graphic representation of the links between all of these elements.

Not all students perceive the course content in the same way. Some provide dynamic connections in maps. Others, like Figure 2.4, are more static but still meaningful. One aspect of the map in Figure 2.4, the interior of a refrigerator, that should be evident to even the casual viewer is the glaring lack of text passages. Nonetheless, the mapmaker has succeeded in representing a wide array of concepts and in linking them meaningfully. Remember that these are not variations on a single essay question. Rather, students must use minimal words and rely on graphics to get their intentions across. (See map directions and a sample rubric later in this chapter.) Although it may seem unusual for a secondary English major to produce a map with the interior of a refrigerator as the metaphor, the focus here should be on the content and the concepts and linkages made between concepts—not on the metaphor by itself.

Using Concept Maps: Setting Up the Assignment

Concept maps can be used to determine formative understandings of content for students at the beginning of a semester or summatively at the end of a semester. When used summatively in my 15-week courses, there are certain requirements that are essential: Students should be introduced to the concept map final examination during the very beginning of the semester (i.e., weeks one and two). They should be aware that they will be required to integrate course content in this project. Hence, I always post approximately 50 maps from previous semesters on the classroom walls and leave them up for about two weeks to provide ample opportunities for walkabout viewing and for questions. The concept map as a final exam, at least in the complex forms I require, is not possible when assigned only at the end of the semester.

Near the end of the semester (i.e., weeks eleven or twelve), students should be required to produce draft maps that start them on the process of thinking about an entire semester of work in reading and the language arts and their content subject major (see map directions in Figure 2.5). Meetings with peers and the course instructor to clarify the meanings and purposes of the author's graphic representations as well as to consider the perceptions of potential

Figure 2.5 Concept Map Final Exam Project

Elementary and Secondary Reading:
A Concept Map Final Exam Project

Some general comments to consider when constructing your concept map for this class:

1. You are to construct a *concept map* which will represent your understanding of what is involved in teaching reading, writing, listening, speaking, viewing, and graphically representing, either in the elementary classroom or across the range of secondary subjects. An article on concept mapping is provided for your use. Read it carefully and consider all the components involved in mapping. Two samples of such maps are included in the handout, but these are quite formal and standard—you should *not* emulate them exactly. You are invited to be creative and original!!

2. Construct your map on a standard sheet of poster board (22 × 28)—a light color or white is preferable. Smaller sizes are also acceptable. Avoid pop-ups, 3–D maps, and maps with protruding objects. You may create your map electronically if you wish.

3. Select a global issue, metaphor, umbrella issue, or theme around which you will organize your map (e.g., Learning to be Literate in Chemistry). Pay particular attention to examples shown to you in class.

4. Consider a range or an array of issues and concepts to build and represent your vision. Suggestions might include factors that influence literacy, parental roles in reading, vocabulary, children's and adolescent literature, various methodologies, study skills/strategies, writing across the curriculum, grouping, textbooks, technology, the role of whole language, assessment, knowledge of child or adolescent development issues, differentiated instruction, multiple intelligences, and so on. This is *not* a complete list, nor is it intended to be. Your course text and other readings can assist you in recalling areas of importance. In a like manner, your field placement experiences and journal responses can play a significant role in refining your thinking and in preparing this visual interpretation of your work as a professional educator.

5. Be sure to provide logical connectives (lines) and justifications (minimal phrases or guiding words—these are active verbs).

---

continued on next page

Figure 2.5 Concept Map Final Exam Project (*cont.*)

6. No group or cooperative maps will be accepted.
7. Students will prepare a rough draft. In class on _____ you will have an opportunity to consult with colleagues and your course instructor about the content and "vision" of your map to make for a more effective final map. These encounters can help you focus on and be more intentional about logical connections and justifications.
8. Feel free to be creative—color code if you like; use geometric shapes, etc. If your symbolism and meaning are not obvious, provide a map key or legend.
9. *Remember*—this map represents *your* understanding of the reading process, its related concepts, its interactions with other disciplines, its role in the life of a productive citizen, and your role in all of this as the teacher/facilitator/decision-maker. This map is an exhibition of your professional understanding of the interconnectedness of the reading and learning processes in promoting literacy across the curriculum.
10. A scoring rubric is provided to guide the construction of your map.
11. Good luck and enjoy!
12. All maps are to be submitted in *two* forms: 1) A hard copy during the regularly scheduled final exam session for this course—TBA. 2) You are to take a digital picture of your map and submit it via Chalk & Wire. Details to follow in class.
13. During the exam session, a process will be announced to guide the sharing of your maps. Time will be set aside for a group consideration of themes and patterns evident in these maps.

viewers are essential in building student confidence for this exam (see Figure 2.6). Students are usually at widely varying levels of comfort and confidence at this stage. The interactions with other students assist them in clarifying their own perspectives and in remembering important components of their knowledge base, which they may have overlooked and may want to include.

Students must have a clear statement of expectations for the map content (see the rubric in Figure 2.7). That said, however, I have found that it is not possible or even advisable

Figure 2.6 Concept Map Rough Draft Work Session

> The focus: Getting feedback from individuals trying to understand your visual communication. You become the viewers of the graphic representations of others.
>
> Join your discipline/subject matter group. Each member of the group should:
>
> 1. Describe the umbrella issue and the major concepts you have selected for emphasis on your concept map final exam. Do these seem to be reasonable in your subject matter area? Do these make sense? What subordinate facets of the map support this theme and arrangement of ideas?
> 2. Discuss whether you have provided appropriate and ample connections and interconnections. Are any relationships unclear? What can be done to improve the viewer's visual awareness of these relationships?
> 3. Have you provided clear and precise words and/or phrases (i.e., active verbs) that explain and justify the connections? Discuss some examples from each map. What could be done to improve these?
> 4. Have you included specifics—that is, if you place assessment as a major concept on your map, do you also list or display specific examples of assessment tools? If you include using literacy strategies in a content subject, do you include specific strategies for doing this in that subject? Carefully assist one another in this area.
> 5. Will the viewer be able to make meaning or sense of this map? Why do you think so?
> 6. Take the feedback you have been given during this session and strive to refine your final product.
>
> A teacher's dilemma: When you conduct sessions that focus on helping all individuals do their very best, there may be many high scores! Does such a project then become a "piece of cake," a worthless exercise? Why or why not? Defend your response(s).

to provide boilerplate directions. Firm parameters within which students must make choices work better than having to assess a class full of maps that are all the same because all map components are rigidly prescribed. Because of this built-in flexibility, I always receive an array of maps that are original, interesting, challenging, and highly informative about the ways in which my students understand important concepts and links. It is also important to remember that while three students may select the same metaphor, for example, a soccer field, the graphic representations of that soccer field and the content placed there are never the same. In the final analysis, this addresses another perpetual problem in college classrooms: plagiarism. The map eliminates most incidences of plagiarism. Word on the street has assured students in my courses that they have to be original, neat, and clear; and although stunning graphics may be eye-catching, the artistry alone never guarantees a good score: It is the content that matters.

Options for Assessing the Concept Map Assignment

A. Individual Presentation and Defense with Course Instructor

While this approach is time consuming and is essentially an oral defense of personal work, it can also be the most effective form of feedback. Students appreciate the opportunity to answer the assessor's questions, clear up misreading of the map, and add verbally to what is already graphically represented. Be sure to plan carefully to provide enough time for each student and for the entire class roster.

B. Presentation in Small Peer Groups and Final Evaluation by Instructor

This option is similar to option A, but it differs in that it engages other students in the assessment process. For my pre-service teachers, who will soon actively do the day-to-day work of assessment, this is a plus. Like option A, it is labor intensive and may not work with tight exam schedules at the end of a semester.

C. Self-Evaluation, Peer Evaluation, and Instructor Evaluation

The beauty of this option is that it requires the producer of the map to first evaluate the product using the rubric then

Figure 2.7 Rubric for Assessing Professional Knowledge About Literacy

Name _____

Criteria	4 Points	3 Points	2 Points	1 Point
Clear theme; umbrella issue, metaphor				
Logical connectives are obvious and plentiful				
Clear justifications, uses active verbs				
Displays an array of literacy concepts				
All six language arts are clearly integrated				
Visual appeal, clarity, and neatness				
Totals				

Note. Comments may be written on the back of this sheet. Be sure to read them.
4 Points: Superior effort, goes well beyond expectations for this assignment.
3 Points: Good effort, met basic expectations.
2 Points: Fair; met some but not all expectations.
1 Point: Weak; demonstrates minimal effort. Note comments about gaps.

to orally present and defend the map with the instructor and a peer, who also provide written feedback on the rubric (see Figure 2.7). Multiple sources of feedback often result in clearer future work and help all participants to clarify their thinking.

D. Presentation Before a Jury of Peers who Grade the Product

It has also been helpful, and entertaining at times, to ask a portion of a class group to present their maps to the entire final exam group. While doing so, a panel of peers also reacts to and completes a rubric for each map. A grand conversation closes the process for each presenter who walks away with multiple completed rubrics on which to ruminate. The instructor remains the final arbiter of the map's efficacy.

E. Public Posting of All Maps at Once

Find a way to display all maps in the examination room all at once. I often just lay them face up on tables. This posting is followed by a walkabout and small or large group discussions of the implications for course content. Final grading is completed by the course instructor. The value of this publication is twofold. It allows all participants in the course to view and consider the points of view and the connections built by peers in the same course during the semester. It also makes for a valuable and public consideration about what constitutes meaningful knowledge from the course during the current semester.

Advantages of the Concept Map

Clearly, using metaphorical concept maps to assess student understanding requires both careful planning and time. Are the maps worth the effort? Yes, concept maps offer several advantages over ordinary papers and tests.

First, concept maps require students to move well beyond factual knowledge. Having graphically displayed what they understand about the course content over the 15-week semester, students can be more confident that they have integrated their knowledge into a meaningful matrix. Second, concept maps require critical thinking and reflection on connections and relationships between concepts and events. Emphasis is on linkages rather than isolated facts. Third, concept maps require students to shift their usual mode of thinking from "Will this be on the test?" to "What do I understand about what I think I know? Can I defend that interpretation?"

Another advantage is that concept maps are difficult to copy; plagiarizing the ideas of others is also minimized—the author must defend and explain what is produced.

Finally, concept maps are effective tools for reflection when used alongside or after traditional testing methods.

Disadvantages of the Concept Map

A discussion of concept mapping would be incomplete, however, if certain drawbacks were not also acknowledged. First, concept maps are time consuming to produce and to evaluate. Second, students can easily perceive the map as a *cute* assignment rather than an exercise in deep thinking. Building in several checkpoints during the semester can mitigate this misperception. Third, the assignment can easily get out of control. Instructors must place firm parameters on the size and materials useable in the map. Students can easily equate size and money invested in materials for the map with excellent critical thinking about course content.

Finally, storage, either physical or electronic, requires space. This requires a commitment to provide either physical space for the actual maps or electronic space for the digital images. Depending on the circumstances, either or both can be appropriate.

Conclusion

What do students think about the concept map final exam, and how does tapping into a student's creativity deepen assessment for them and for the instructor? After completing the concept map final exam, students are offered an opportunity to anonymously explain how the mapping exercise helped them clarify what they know and understand about teaching in the secondary content subjects with a strong focus on literacy, or in the elementary classroom. Representative student responses to the question "How did this map assignment help you consolidate your thinking about teaching and learning?" follow.

The map has caused me to consider the intricacies of meaning and how they affect literacy. I know that being literate is crucial to the learning of biological concepts, and that unless both teacher and student work towards it, literacy will be difficult to achieve. (Biology major)

It forced me to look for connections between words and concepts. It made me look at the big picture. I know that mathematics has a language specific to itself. I know that literacy is not merely something for English teachers to worry about or to concentrate on, but rather it's for all teachers, including math teachers. (Math major)

It reminded me how important groundwork is to the ability to move upward. The map also forced me to be reflective on topics in a way I would not have considered on my own. Literacy is key in English and it is important to see that teachers and students are successful through literacy in the classroom. (English major)

I wrestled with the connections, what was most important (I couldn't include everything), carrying the metaphor through, and when to finally stop and declare it finished. Literacy is so much more than reading and writing, and it is vitally important to learning. Very soon I will be applying all of these ideas in my classroom (a scary and exciting idea) in order to produce scientifically literate students. (Biology major)

The map helped me because if we are able to make our own decisions on what we are going to teach, how we are going to assess, or what materials we'll use . . . then we will be able to defend ourselves and convey our convictions on what is most important for students to learn. I've become a decision maker and this map surely shows that. (Kinesiology major)

The design of the map demanded choices and prioritizing. The reality helped my reflection and analysis because I had the freedom and duty to choose what I thought was pertinent. (English major)

This map has been helpful by forcing me to think of the bigger picture instead of just the individual components. I had to work carefully to completely understand each attribute to fit them together. (Music education major)

The concept map forced me to synthesize all the information I learned in this class as well as all of my PK in order to put it all together and form real, meaningful connections between various ideas. It also required me to review all of the information and analyze it separately to determine if I wanted to include it on the map. (English major)

The map helped me to make meaningful and logical connections between what I felt in my gut and what I could produce on paper—which is different than the picture in my head. (History major)

For teachers who are prepared to take the long, slow approach to concept mapping in general and to metaphorical mapping in particular, the rewards can be immense. A new colleague of mine was so intrigued by the mapping alternative to final exams that she offered to collaborate with me on the assignment during her first year at the college. In a personal email communication, she states:

Using metaphorical concept maps in my secondary reading methods class was an eye-opening experience for me. Students engaged in the process of identifying a metaphor, selecting important course content, making connections between big ideas, and then justifying those connections and fitting all that thoughtfully within their metaphor. In order to do this, students struggled and revisited the big ideas from the course a number of times. They also engaged in dialogue with their classmates. I was privy to these struggles and conversations, as well as the drafts of the maps as they were being developed. I also conversed with a number of students individually. Having this additional data helped me understand each student's finished map with more clarity and also revealed the depth of understanding (or misunderstanding) that each student possessed. I was amazed at the sophistication of many of the concept maps, and felt that, as a summative assessment, this was a great assignment. There is no way I could have learned as much about what each student knew and could do through a multiple choice or essay exam. In addition, students were able to demonstrate the connections between learning, teaching, literacy, and pedagogy in a way that is usually unmeasurable in a methods class. I will definitely use metaphorical concept maps as an assessment tool in future classes. (L. Pardo, June 29, 2006)

In the final analysis, I will continue to use concept maps alongside traditional exams and quizzes to assess what students in my courses know and understand about content. The mapping exercise stretches students' abilities, requires them to demonstrate deep understanding in new ways, and, in the end, makes them more appreciative of what it is they actually do know and understand. I sense they become more confident, more articulate, and clearer about personal competencies as a result. Alone, the maps might mean little. Paired with the many experiences they encounter throughout their programs of study, the maps enhance and deepen understanding and professional dispositions.

References

Rafferty, C. D., & Fleschner, L. K. (1993, Spring). Concept mapping: A viable alternative to objective and essay exams. *Reading Research and Instruction, 33*(3), 25–34.

3

Getting Creative in a Required Course: Variable Grading, Learning Logs, and Authentic Testing

Barbara A. Mezeske

"Students learn best when they are engaged." "Active learning engages students' thinking." "Engagement is the key to motivation." Over and over again, we hear the word *engaged* used to describe the best student learning. But how do we engage students and overcome that passivity so many of them bring to the classroom? Particularly, how do we do that in required or core curriculum classes?

My approach to this problem in a core curriculum literature class has been to involve students in the assessment of their learning by giving them a range of choices about how they demonstrate what they know, by asking them to reflect on their learning in explicit ways, and by testing them about material I have not taught. Each of these strategies requires students to make meaningful decisions that affect the outcome of the course: The result is engagement.

Background

Western World Literature II is one of a battery of courses that can satisfy the "cultural heritage" requirement at Hope College. It is not required of English majors, though occasionally some do show up on the rolls. Because the cultural heritage courses always involve a significant amount of reading, they are frequently the last core courses that non-humanities majors select. And because they are often underenrolled when our first-year students register, many of them select it as well. Thus, the class is made up of a variety of students—freshmen to seniors—with a range of disciplinary interests.

While the official goal of the course is to introduce students to "masterpieces of the Western tradition since the Renaissance," the course needed something more to satisfy its audience of non-majors. To the official goal, therefore, I added this: "to learn to read literature with deep understanding, and maybe even with love." This seems to be a sensible and worthwhile goal because most of the reading that people will do as adults will be for pleasure, not because some instructor has assigned it, lectured on it, and written a test. L. Dee Fink (2003) poses this question when he speaks of what faculty want from course design:

> In your deepest, fondest dreams, what kind of impact would you most like to have on your students? That is, when the course is over and it is now one or two years later, what would you like to be true about students who have had your courses that is not true of others? (p. 9)

My dream for this course is that it will equip students to read new texts with enjoyment and sophistication for the rest of their lives.

Engaging Students: Variable Grading

The first and most radical change I made in my course design was to adopt variable grading. Variable grading requires professors to write a menu of possible ways for students to demonstrate what they know about the subject matter. The menu has to be extensive in order to allow real choice, and each activity on the menu must in some way measure the cognitive and affective goals of the course. I generally write about 1,000 points of possible activities and require about 450 to pass the course. Each activity is worth a certain number of points, roughly indicative of the amount of work it requires. A test, for example, is worth 50 points; a one-page paper is worth 10. A typical menu includes conventional tests, one-page essays, five- to six-page essays, and learning logs. (Other choices might include in-class presentations, group or individual projects, attendance or participation in out-of-class activities, or service assignments.) I also write daily, 10-point, objective quizzes over the reading that must be taken by every student in class on a particular day. Given the nature of the course, I have found that quizzes ensure that students come to class prepared to discuss the reading. Most students see the quizzes, quite realistically, as an evil necessity. In a mid-semester learning log, a student wrote,

> I have gotten used to taking quizzes every day for this class. It is an acquired habit like expecting to be picked on in Japanese class or assuming [the cafeteria] is serving food I would label as "not good." . . . I do not mind taking quizzes every day because it no longer has the element of surprise nor the word "pop" associated with it.

In an end-of-semester course evaluation, another student wrote, "I like the quizzes because they are a consistent way to earn points and really encourage me to do the reading."

Maryellen Weimer (2002) offers an extensive discussion of the effects of having students decide what assignments they will complete to demonstrate what they know. She concludes that "Learner-centered instruction involves a reallocation of power in the classroom. It requires that faculty give students some control over those learning processes that directly affect them" (p. 45). Ceding control to students is not easy to those of us accustomed to making all of the important decisions in a classroom, especially the decision about how students demonstrate mastery of our learning objectives. Students know this, too. One student wrote on his first learning log, "When faced with the option of choosing how I would earn my points, I was at first a bit stunned. For the first time in my academic career, I was going to fashion my own learning plan!" Another student wrote, "No other course that I have taken at college comes even remotely close to giving students as much control over their grade." Of course, one might argue that students *always* have control over how and when they study, over how much time they spend on an assignment, over how they schedule and complete lengthy assignments. But variable grading takes that a step further by asking students to decide *what* assignments to complete, thereby jerking them awake to the fact that they, not the teacher, have real, discretionary control of what they do.

Two assumptions undergird the decision to give students the power to choose how they are evaluated. First, it is not necessary for all students to do the same activities to learn or to demonstrate learning. Second, it is not necessary for them to do activities at the same times. Both assumptions are grounded in the reality that students are not identical: They come to our classes with different strengths and weaknesses and different learning styles. As John C. Bean (1996) notes,

> At perhaps no time in history have college professors faced a more diverse group of students than at present. At many institutions, students have such a wide range of backgrounds, aptitudes, and academic preparation that teachers hardly know where to pitch instruction. (p. 38)

How then can we expect to measure what each of them knows using only a single kind of measuring tool? And when we recognize that different measures of achievement are a good idea, it is only a short step to allowing those measurements to take place at various times during the semester.

How does this work in practice? In a variable grading system, there are due dates for every activity: Without them, students would procrastinate and bury the instructor with work to evaluate in the last week of the course. Due dates help everyone to distribute work sensibly over the duration of a course. One benefit of variable grading is that a professor need no longer face large piles of papers, tests, and journals all due from everyone on the same day. Instead, because students choose from a range of assignments that have due dates distributed throughout the semester, the instructor's workload is similarly distributed in a steady stream. Moreover, there is no makeup work. When a due date has passed, an assignment can no longer be submitted. Students who are absent for quizzes or tests must make up those points in some other way. Finally, every assignment is evaluated according to a rubric available to students in advance. Thus, merely attempting the required number of points is no guarantee of success in the course. Variable grading gives students choices, but still holds them accountable for the quality of their work.

This is all unfamiliar territory to most students, and they need some coaching to succeed. To help students, I encourage them to make a game plan in the first two weeks. In the game plan, they project how they will demonstrate to me what they have learned. I ask them to reflect on what skills and understandings each kind of assignment will require, what skills and understandings they already possess, and which need to be polished. I also ask them to consider which tasks will be most interesting. Finally, I ask them to consider the other courses they are taking and how the workload in those courses is distributed. I point out that variable grading allows them to concentrate their work for my class during weeks when other classes do not have major exams or papers.

Another way to help students manage the freedom to choose assignments is to keep them apprised of where they stand. I use an Excel spreadsheet to keep track of attempted and earned points, and I report point counts regularly to students. It is especially important to keep an eye on the "point of no return" when there are no longer enough points available for a student to earn the required number to pass the course. One could adjust this system further, dividing the semester into quarters or thirds, and requiring a certain number of attempted points during each segment of the semester.

Engaging Students: Reflection on Their Learning

A second important component of students' experience in this course—and a key to assessing student learning—is the learning log. Learning logs are short, one-page reflections on some aspect of students' personal learning. They are not journals or diaries nor are they merely "responses." At best, when students write about something they have learned, their learning log "reinforces that learning and directs attention to the learning processes themselves" (Weimer, 2002, p. 65). I evaluate learning logs according to the rubric shown in Figure 3.1.

Figure 3.1 Learning Log Rubric

Clarity	Expresses a clear point of view in an organized manner. Uses literary terms where appropriate.
Correctness	Attends to the conventions of grammar, spelling, usage, mechanics, and syntax.
Specificity	Answers the question(s) using clear examples and illustrations.
Sophistication	Gives evidence of awareness of controversy, alternatives to and complexities of concepts and issues.
Synthesis	Provides connections between course content (both reading and discussion) and *other* experiences (academic or personal).

There is a wide variety of possible topics for learning logs, including these:

- Make a game plan for how you will earn points in this course.
- Describe what you do when you read and the kind of reading experiences you have had.
- Take a passage handed out in class. Read it several times, then describe what you notice about its vocabulary, tone, and meaning. Predict what the rest of the work will be like.
- Reread the syllabus (late in the semester) and comment on an element of the course design that has affected your learning in a positive or negative way.
- Describe how you prepare for an exam. What strategies do you use? Have they been successful in the past?
- Choose two important things you have learned in the course. What are they, and why are they important?

Other learning log topics can be more content specific. I have, for example, assessed students' understanding of romanticism by asking them if they consider themselves to be romantics or realists.

By asking students to think and write explicitly about how or what they have learned, teachers can assess their course designs and what students gain from them in the most practical and direct way imaginable: by listening to students. In addition, by writing about their own experiences in the class, students come to a better assessment of their own learning and its integration into their identities. In a final learning log, one student wrote:

> The most important thing I learned in this course was everything about myself. Somehow, throughout this course and its discussion of different [literary] themes, I found myself aligning with some, shunning others, wholeheartedly embracing a few

as well as realizing I was not exactly what I thought I was.

Of course, sometimes the learning logs reflect a less happy experience:

> I had always thought of myself as a person who gets things done right promptly, but I have come to find out that is only because I was forced to do all of the assignments. I realized that I need to put more effort into my assignments instead of just completing them. I realized I have to be more disciplined with myself to learn new information and use it in my work.

In short, it is the learning logs that allow me to write this chapter and to make the assertions I have made about students' learning. I have discovered that students are not asked often enough to comment on their own learning or on the effectiveness of various classroom strategies. When such opportunities for reflection take place in limited, end-of-semester course evaluations, there is little reason for students to be reflective or thoughtful because nothing they say will change anything. However, when we ask students to think and write about our courses while they are in progress, we find that they are full of helpful suggestions and criticisms, and they are remarkably honest in reporting the effect of our practices on their learning. By using learning logs, we invite our students into the conversation about learning, and we acknowledge their stake in what we do together.

Engaging Students: Authentic Testing

If my goal in this course is for students "to learn to read literature with deep understanding, and maybe even with love," and if the learning logs give me a window into students *affective* response to the course, then I need a way to assess their cognitive growth: Do they, in fact, develop skills that enable them to deeply understand what they read? Of course, I could simply administer tests over all the literature we had considered as a group. Such tests could measure their recall of important terms and concepts and their ability to make connections between different works. But what I *really* wanted to know about my students and about the course I designed was whether or not they could read a new piece of literature on their own and emerge with a fairly sophisticated understanding of it.

The tests I administer are over medium length works of literature: poems of at least 40 lines or short stories of about 20 pages. I have used, for example, Tennyson's "Ulysses," D. H. Lawrence's "The Horse Dealer's Daughter," and Joyce Carol Oates's "Did You Ever Slip on Red Blood?" About a week before the test, I pass out copies of the work the test will cover. Most students take the handout even if they do not intend to take the test. This is encouraging: It suggests that they read the work and think about whether they want to take the test, thus demonstrating an important kind of engagement with the course. Once the students have the test material in hand, they may mark and annotate it any way they please. I help them by giving them a handout that summarizes what any good reader does when confronted with a new text (see Figure 3.2).

On the day of the test, students come to class armed with their annotated copies of the test material. The test questions are arranged in a hierarchy of sophistication, roughly parallel to Bloom's taxonomy of learning outcomes (Woolfolk, 2001). The first questions might ask students to identify characters or explain elements of the plot. The next questions might ask them to address issues of style by focusing on the word choice in a particular paragraph or on the way a writer has organized a work. There might be a reference to a specific passage (e.g., "Note the way

Figure 3.2 Test Preparation Guidelines

How to Prepare for the Tests

1. Read the work you will be tested on. Reread it. Reread especially parts that seem critical to understanding. (See below.)
2. As you read, take note of unfamiliar vocabulary. This is *crucial* with poetry, but also important in prose. In *The Metamorphosis*, Gregor Samsa wakes up to find "himself changed in his bed into a monstrous vermin." Unless you know that "vermin" means "various small animals or insects such as rats or cockroaches that are destructive, annoying, or injurious to health,"* you will miss the point.

   The American Heritage Dictionary of the English Language 4th ed. Online: www.bartleby .com/61/
3. Note the beginning. What is the mood of the first line or first sentence? How does the writer choose to draw in the reader? Is something happening? Or is there a description?
4. Note the ending. Is some point made, either explicitly or implicitly? Or is the point left unresolved, up to the reader to figure out? Is the ending abrupt, surprising? Or does it resolve the threads of the plot?
5. Pay attention to the point of view. What pronouns are used? Who is speaking? Try to decide what the speaker or storyteller knows: Everything? Or just some things?
6. Imagine an outline of the work. Note the order of events or images. Think about why the writer structured the piece in this way.
7. Look for literary elements, especially those we have addressed in class: satire, irony, symbolism, imagery, comedy. Don't forget setting, plot, and character.
8. If there are characters, form opinions about them. What motivates them? What are their strengths and weaknesses?
9. Make a personal response to the reading. Do you identify with anything in the text? Are elements of your personal experience or culture reflected in the work?
10. Connect the work to a larger context. What does it have in common with other works we have studied as a class? How does it compare or contrast to those other works? Does it have a similar theme or meaning? Are the characters alike or different? Is the language similar or different?
11. Connect the work to a still larger thematic context. Does this work comment on the themes we address in this class (identity, relationships and gender, natural world, power)? Does it have other meanings?
12. Make notes. Many good readers mark up their texts. Others use notebooks. Underline sparingly. Pose questions in the margins.

---

the point of view shifts in the third paragraph on page 12. Where else does Oates do this sort of shifting, and how does it affect you as a reader?"). More sophisticated questions ask about character, theme, and the qualities of the work that correspond to or differ from the generalized characteristics of the literary periods we have studied in class. The final question is always something like this: "Do you have any additional observation about this text that has not been covered in the preceding questions? Is there anything that you wish to add?" By asking this, I am acknowledging that, in their study of the work over the past week, students may have reached some insight or understanding that I have not covered in my questions. I am often surprised, and pleased, when a student helps me to see a story or poem in a new light. Moreover, it is important to acknowledge, even on a test, that the instructor does not "own" the meaning of a work of literature: Individual readers make their own meaning, and it should be honored.

Students' Assessment of the Course

Not every student is happy with these strategies. In particular, students who are habitual procrastinators can suffer. Given the power to decide what assignments to attempt, many attempt none at all. Their passivity with regard to their education is firmly entrenched, and it takes much prodding to get them to begin to make decisions and take action. Most of them come around, like this student who commented in an end-of-course learning log,

> The most important thing that I feel I have learned is how to better organize my time. In this class I did not do that. I left most everything for the last half of the class. I somehow finished with just enough points, but it was getting pretty close.

In five years of experimenting with this course design, I have had to make specific assignments and deadlines for a student only once; she was a bright individual with lots of personal issues and just could not cope with the freedom. After I told her which papers and tests she *had* to do, and *when* to turn them in, she was able to complete the course.

Most students, however, like this design. They make comments like these:

> Overall this system of choice has been very effective. It forces responsibility, organization, and hard work. . . . Not only does it help foster learning, but it helps students recognize the ways in which they learn best.

> Overall, I have learned that I need to take more initiative for myself to learn all that I want. I can no longer rely on the teacher to provide all of that for me, like I did in high school. This course has taught me things that I will carry with me throughout the rest of my life.

> This course is one of the few I took this year that helped me to develop my thinking process. Not only do I now know more, but also I know how to know more. This course helped me to get my life in order.

Conclusion

Getting one's life in order. Now, that is not usually a goal that I would include on my syllabus. However, when one considers the purposes of higher education, is not "getting one's life in order" just about as important as our more conventional goals that address what students will know and what skills they will develop?

The ultimate value of the kind of creative assessment I practice is this: It engages students directly and explicitly in the decision-making that goes into their learning. Every element of course design addressed in this chapter—variable grading, learning logs, and authentic testing—is aimed at making learning an active rather than a passive act. Variable grading gives students real choices about how they will demonstrate their learning. Learning logs ask students to reflect explicitly on what and how they have learned. Authentic testing gives students opportunities to practice the skills that the course intends to impart. Taken together, all three make it possible for teacher and student to know what it is they have learned. And that is the most meaningful kind of assessment, after all.

References

Bean, J. C. (1996). *Engaging ideas: The professor's guide to integrating writing, critical thinking, and active learning in the classroom.* San Francisco, CA: Jossey-Bass.

Fink, L. D. (2003). *Creating significant learning experiences: An integrated approach to designing college courses.* San Francisco, CA: Jossey-Bass.

Weimer, M. (2002). *Learner-centered teaching: Five key changes to practice.* San Francisco, CA: Jossey-Bass.

Woolfolk, A. (2001). *Educational psychology.* Boston, MA: Allyn & Bacon.

4

"From Now on You'll Be History": The Transition from Memorization to Analysis

Janis M. Giibbs

Both students and teachers in college history classes face challenges to their skills, their understandings, and their expectations. In high school, most students learn to use textbooks and to think of history as a series of dates, names, events, and narratives. This type of teaching in the schools has been shaped, since the 1980s at least, by debates over the content and the goals of history courses. What should students know? What skills should they develop? While exceptions certainly exist, especially in schools with honors courses or advanced placement programs, most pre-college teaching in the early 1990s focused on the acquisition of a basic fund of content knowledge that could be tested (Stearns, 1994). As a result of this pedagogical development, many students arrive in college without a clear sense of what a college history course requires. Many expect to learn dates and names and a chronological narrative without having to think about interpretation or analysis. The emphasis on data collection and factual narrative that many students bring from high school collides with the expectations of faculty at the college level.

College faculty tend to expect a greater degree of historical sophistication from students than most freshmen and sophomores are able to demonstrate. In a British study of faculty and student perspectives on the transition from school to university history courses, faculty saw students as possessing narrow interests, mostly focused on the 20th century (Booth, 2005). The faculty thought that students placed more confidence in their ability to collect data than to construct analyses of their own, relied too heavily on textbooks and teachers' notes, lacked the sense of history as a changing, analytical understanding of the past, lacked skills in research, writing, grammar, spelling, numeracy and languages, and focused too heavily on examination results rather than on learning (Booth, 2005). The perceptions revealed by Booth's British study match, to a large degree, the unscientific observations of the faculty at our small liberal arts college in Michigan. In response to a general sense of frustration about trying to teach students the skills of historical analysis—how to think, read, and write like a historian—our small (7.5 full-time positions) history department revised our program in the late 1990s to require an introductory course of all history majors and minors. To avoid scaring students away, we chose not to call the course "historiography." Instead, we called it "History Workshop" to emphasize that the course would require students to participate in a series of activities and exercises designed to build their foundation of skills as historians. This change represented a significant alteration to our previous major and minor, which consisted of distribution requirements but not particular courses or sequences of courses. In the old system, majors and minors were required to take one United States history course, one course in history before 1500 CE, one course in European history after 1500, one course in non-Western or global history, and four elective courses. Majors were, in addition, required to take a capstone seminar course in which they wrote a significant original research paper.

Our experience indicated that many students reached the capstone seminar without a clear sense of how to write a research paper. Because the loose structure of the major meant that there was no required sequence of courses, there was no place where we could be sure students would learn the basics of historical research and analysis before their senior year. The addition of the History Workshop addressed this problem by defining a place in the curriculum where students could learn and practice basic research and writing skills. In the History Workshop, students would learn to analyze primary sources, read and understand historical arguments, and conduct basic historical research. As it was initially conceived, the course did not include the writing of a final research paper, but in response to early student feedback, we added a final research paper to the requirements and designed many (but not all) of the course's workshop sessions to serve as steps in the process of writing the paper. While some students delay taking the History Workshop, ideally students take it as sophomores as soon as they decide to become history majors or minors. The purpose of the course is to provide students with a better transition from high school history courses to college history courses and to prepare students for the demands of higher-level history courses. In particular, we aim to teach students that the really interesting and significant part of historical studies is analysis. We include units on working with both primary and secondary sources, reading scholarly articles, reading monographs, conducting library research, constructing annotated bibliographies, and writing a medium-length research paper (8–12 pages). The course varies in its subject matter depending on which faculty member teaches it. In general, it alternates between American history and European history because the faculty in those areas are able to incorporate the course into their teaching rotations more easily than the fewer faculty who teach global (non-Western) courses.

In teaching the History Workshop on a European history topic, we encountered another challenge. Many of our students have had little or no exposure to history other than American history. Most of our students attended high school in Michigan. Until changes enacted in 2006, Michigan did not require students to take any history courses in high school. Beginning with the high school class of 2011, Michigan will require all high school students to take three credits in social studies, including half a credit in civics, half a credit in economics, one credit in United States history and geography, and one credit in world history and geography (Michigan Department of Education, 2006). While individual schools (and schools outside of Michigan) might have different requirements, the general result of the lack of consistent history requirements in the schools is an annual cohort of new history majors whose experience with history courses varies widely, from students who have had no history classes since middle school to students who completed highly sophisticated, advanced placement courses. Our experience is that the students with limited exposure to history courses in high school outnumber the students whose exposure demonstrates breadth, depth, or both.

As a result of their varied preparation, many students think they have no knowledge about the subject and therefore they are reluctant to offer their ideas and interpretations either in discussions or in written work. Many students also suspect that everybody else in the class knows more than they do. This is not an atmosphere conducive to active and effective learning. It is particularly difficult to engage students in useful analytical discussion when they feel as though they do not know anything about the subject. As a result, we looked for ways to engage students in a discussion that would introduce them to the kinds of analysis we expect in college history courses, without demanding that they possess significant knowledge about history, without being patronizing or boring, and without alienating the students who did have more experience with history courses. With this set of goals, what is a professor to do?

The Exercise: Assessing Students' Understanding of Historical Analysis

The first time we offered the History Workshop, the topic was "The European Witch Hunt of the 16th and 17th Centuries." This topic was manageable because it provided a tight focus with a great deal of recent scholarship, a good supply of published primary sources, and a variety of interpretations for students to consider. It was, though, a topic with which most students were unfamiliar. Since then, we have broadened the topic to "Religion, Politics, and Society in Europe, 1500–1800," but the course still presents students with a time period and a selection of topics with which they are unfamiliar. To demystify the unfamiliar topic and to provide students with a challenging but nonintimidating assignment at the beginning of the course, we developed an exercise in which students receive a packet of "primary source documents." These documents are not real documents; we created them to serve the purpose of the exercise. The packet contains a series of related bits of information, including newspaper articles, classified ads, weather reports, mortality and morbidity tables, a handwritten, intentionally illegible receipt, and a map. The first step in the assignment is for students, working in groups, to figure out what the unifying event reflected in the documents is. To make the assignment possible for students who had little or no exposure to European history, we chose a fictional event with which many students would be familiar: the death of the Witch of the East from the movie version of *The Wizard of Oz*.

The documents present a series of challenges for students. In the first document, a series of weather reports, students encounter a table with unlabeled columns, shown in Figure 4.1.

The first column contains dates. Students might be able to guess this, and by using information from other documents in the packet, they can confirm that the first column contains dates. The dates are simply invented. Month names are modified from the French revolutionary calendar. (*Brumaire*, the windy month, became *Brumot*. The wind turns out to be significant, but the students do not know that until later in the exercise.) The third column contains temperature readings, but they are irrelevant to the problem

Figure 4.1 Weather Reports

Weather Reports Weather Station ML Brumot 1–15, 900		
Brumot 1	Rainy	20
Brumot 2	Hail	17
Brumot 3	Hail, clearing late in day	18
Brumot 4	Sunny	22
Brumot 5	Sunny	24
Brumot 6	Partially sunny; wind rising late in day	20
Brumot 7	Cloudy	19
Brumot 8	West wind rising	17
Brumot 9	Sunny	22
Brumot 10	Windy	20
Brumot 11	Changeable	21
Brumot 12	Pressure falling, precipitation likely at night and in early morning hours	15
Brumot 13	Stormy weather in early morning hours, precipitation likely; clear day to follow. Breeze from North	16
Brumot 14	Clear skies: East wind	16
Brumot 15	Rainy	17

in the packet. Neither the dates nor the temperature readings, nor most of the weather descriptions come from the real *Wizard of Oz*. From this document alone, the students cannot be expected to figure out anything about the assignment. It is only by reading the document in connection with other documents that the relevant material becomes clear. This helps students see the value of reading sources in connection with each other.

Figure 4.2 contains the "Statutes of the Lollipop Guild." Once again, these are pure invention, created to make a point. By reading the statutes, students might learn significant details about costuming, gender structures, culture and customs, and the money system in the society under

Figure 4.2 Statutes of the Lollipop Guild

A. Each Brother shall provide a new suit of guild clothing annually. Each suit shall consist of a pair of short pants with handkerchief hems, in an official Guild color, striped hose, Elfin boots, and a suitable jacket.

B. Brothers who are unable to afford a new suit annually shall have a suit provided them from the coffers of the guild.

C. Each Brother must attend the monthly guild banquet and take responsibility as a member of the guild for provision of provender for the banquet once a year.

D. Guild banquets shall consist of a savory soup, a crunchy salad, a bean dish, well-cooked, a roast, a fowl, a fish, a cheese, and a soft sweet. Hard sweets of the Guild manufacture shall be provided at the end of every banquet.

E. Guild dues are three silver Munkets annually, or 25 copper pennigs. Dues are payable at the Annual Lollipop Festival.

F. Brothers shall give all assistance to each other in cases of illness, inability to work, and cases of particular need.

G. All Brothers shall dance a Guild dance at the wedding or funeral of a member, at the birth of a son to a member of the Guild, and on suitable public occasions.

H. Sons of Brothers shall, in due course, be invited to take up membership in the Guild. Sons-in-law may join the Guild upon a vote of approval by a simple majority of the Membership.

I. Widows of Brothers carry auxiliary membership, but may not vote in Guild elections.

J. The chief Guild officer is the Stick, elected annually by a simple majority vote of the members. The Stick shall appoint a council to help him govern the affairs of the Guild. A Brother must have been a member in good standing for five years in order to be eligible for election as the Stick. A Brother must have been a member in good standing for two years to serve on the council.

K. The Guild may, at the discretion of the Stick and the Council, present a ceremonial Lollipop to deserving members of the community.

L. Brothers who break the regulations of the Guild shall be spat out.

M. Brothers who have improper dealings with the current irregular authorities shall be spat out.

N. [This paragraph is blank on purpose in the copy students see.]

consideration. There is a hint, in paragraph M, of political unrest. The statutes also contain a lettered paragraph (paragraph N) that has no content. This suggests that the document might be incomplete.

By the time students finish Figure 4.2, some of them have started to think about *The Wizard of Oz* because of the reference to the Lollipop Guild. Others are still confused about the event that unifies the documents. Student discussion often becomes lively at this point as students look at the remaining documents with an eye to testing their hypothesis about *The Wizard of Oz*.

The third document the students encounter is the "Official Register of Mortality and Morbidity, Office of the Coroner, Brumot 10–15, 900" (see Figure 4.3). This chart, unlike the weather table, has labeled columns, and students can use the two together to figure out that Brumot must be a month with the day following. Further, they can correlate deaths with the weather and conclude that in at least one case, a victim died when the weather was bad.

The "Official Register" is intentionally filled with irrelevant information concerning deaths of characters not appearing in *The Wizard of Oz*. Some students can readily identify characters from other literary works and popular culture sources (*Gulliver's Travels, Candide,* a children's song, *Oklahoma!,* and *Romeo and Juliet*). Along with the other clues about *The Wizard of Oz*, this table helps them narrow their focus to the death of Hecate, a witch, who was crushed to death on Brumot 14. On the day of her death, not coincidentally, there was "stormy weather in [the] early morning hours, likely precipitation and a clear day to follow," with a "breeze from the North." Students with a good memory for song lyrics might notice that the "degrees" of death parallel those listed in "Ding, Dong, the Witch is Dead," from *The Wizard of Oz* ("Not only is she merely dead/ She's really most sincerely dead"; Fleming, 1939).

By the time they finish with the "Official Register of Mortality and Morbidity," most students are on a mission

Figure 4.3 Official Register of Mortality and Morbidity

Official Register of Mortality and Morbidity
Office of the Coroner
Brumot 10—15, 900

Name	Occupation	Date of Death	Cause	Degree
Lemuel Gulliver	Ship's Physician	Brumot 10	Collapsed under severe body weight; pathological gigantism	Reliably
Pangloss	Doctor	Brumot 10	Unidentified wasting disease	Apparently
Eddie Brown	Student	Brumot 11	Fell into the well; drowned	Really
Camille	Unemployed	Brumot 11	Consumption	Thoroughly
Judd Frye	Farmer	Brumot 12	Hanged himself up from a rope in the smokehouse	Merely
Hecate	Witch	Brumot 13	Crushed	Most Sincerely
Juliet Capulet	Virgin (reported by parents; not reliable medical conclusion)	Brumot 14	Swooned with fever; subsequently stabbed; suspicion of suicide	Undeniably

to find out what else supports their hypothesis about *The Wizard of Oz*. The next document, shown in Figure 4.4, contains a series of news reports and an advertisement.

From these reports, students learn that there is a news source called the "EC Chronicle," though they cannot, from this document, figure out what "EC" means. They learn that there is some kind of polity with an elected mayor and some kind of a judiciary system. The news reports suggest a causal relationship between the stormy weather in the East and the death of Hecate, which was reflected in the "Official Register of Mortality and Morbidity." "Reliable, unnamed sources in the North" is a reference to Glinda; students who are on the trail of *The Wizard of Oz* suspect

Figure 4.4 News Reports and Advertisements

From News Reports

22 Thermot, 899, Dom Perignon, a portly fellow in a green jacket and trousers, was reelected to the Big Hat today, as he won the two hundred and seventy-second Mayoral election. Perignon, who has been Mayor for the past twelve years, said that he was happy to win again, as he was just getting comfortable with balancing the hat, which stands half as high as he does, on his head for ceremonial occasions. He will be sworn in by Chief Justice Rehnqbridge, who has promised to sew new gold racing strips on his red judicial robe for the occasion.

From News Reports

EC Chronicle, 15 Brumot, 900. Rumors have reached the City of great disturbances in the order of things in the world. Stormy weather in the East is reported to have resulted in the sudden death of Hecate, the de facto ruler of the East. An uprising among the people of the East has also been reported; these reports are unsubstantiated. It is possible that a new power is abroad in the land.

Reliable, unnamed sources in the North, who claim to have been present shortly after the alleged cataclysmic events in the East, have confirmed the passing of Hecate, but have refused to speculate about the identity of the agent of Hecate's destruction. The alleged new power has disappeared from the East suddenly, and nobody is quite sure where this new power—wizard? witch? sorceress?—is headed.

From the Classified Ads

EC Chronicle, 14 Brumot 900. Lost: One pair shoes, red. Family heirloom. Looted from estate of deceased sister. Reward. Shoes are dangerous. Do not try to use them yourself. Contact the Winkies in the West to collect reward.

---

this, but cannot support their hypothesis with evidence from the documents. This gives them an opportunity to use prior knowledge and to hypothesize about details not clearly stated in the sources. The reference to Hecate as "the de facto ruler of the East" suggests illegitimacy in Hecate's rule; if students remember the Munchkins' celebration at the witch's death, they can begin to put together the political context of the East. Of course, they do not yet know about people called "Munchkins"; it is useful to remind them again that prior knowledge and hypothetical connections are important, but documentation is also a significant part of historical analysis.

Finally, the classified advertisement, seeking the return of "one pair shoes, red. Family heirloom. Looted from estate of deceased sister," gives the students a hint that a deceased person has a sister, who is interested in the recovery of property. Students may remember the Witch of the West and her desire for the ruby slippers, but that much detail cannot be gleaned from these documents.

The next document in the packet is a handwritten, purposefully illegible receipt for "one pr. striped hose, black/white, size 8." It contains a price (1 M 4 pen.) and a scrawled signature, which no student yet has deciphered as the professor's. This document gives the students experience reading illegible handwriting and being frustrated by their inability to figure out what it says and how it fits. Those who figure out what it says and remember the film note that it is possible that the receipt reflects a purchase either by Hecate or by a member of the Lollipop Guild because both Guild members and the Witch of the East wore striped stockings. Ambiguity can be a frustrating part of historical research.

The final document in the packet, not reproduced here, is a map, taken from an edition of L. Frank Baum's *The Wizard of Oz*. It depicts a square land, not labeled as Oz, but showing the Gillikins in the north, the Munchkins in the East, the Quadlings in the South, and the Winkies in the West. The Emerald City is labeled in the middle, and the yellow brick road is barely discernable, running from the starred capital of the Munchkins to the Emerald City. The land is bordered on all four sides by desert (Hearn, 2000). This document in combination with the others provides persuasive evidence that the packet deals with an event from *The Wizard of Oz*.

The document exercise proceeds with students in small groups examining the documents and responding to a discussion guide with four prompts (see Figure 4.5).

The exercise has a double significance. First, students exercise their skills at analysis and interpretation. Second, they are required to reflect on the way they think about historical sources. The prompts ask the students to consider not only what they can learn from the documents, but what they cannot learn from them. Figuring out what questions they might ask next is an important skill for students to develop and is an important part of the transition from high school history classes to college history classes. Instead of answering questions provided by the professor, students can begin to formulate their own questions. This is one of the first steps in teaching students how to formulate interesting questions for their own papers. The questions they raise range from "What is the gender structure of the society described in the documents?" to "What was Hecate crushed by?" to "What does the article mean when it says the 'de facto ruler of the

Figure 4.5 First Written Sources Discussion Guide

Learning from Written Sources, Exercise One

1. Examine the written sources. What questions do they present? What don't you understand? Why? What problems do you have with the sources?
2. Can you figure out what event links these sources? What is it? How do you know?
3. Do you have any background knowledge that assists you in your interpretation of the written sources?
4. What was most helpful to you in interpreting this collection of sources?

East'?" Students can expand their discussion by considering what kinds of sources might give them the information they need to answer their questions. Some questions, such as "What was Hecate crushed by?" are more or less factual; others require more analysis. By looking at the kinds of questions they ask, students begin to see that there are different kinds of historical questions and different goals of research.

After the students have had a chance to consider the sources, figure out that a witch was crushed to death during a windstorm, and perhaps identify the story as *The Wizard of Oz*, the exercise moves on to a second part. We distribute a second discussion guide shown in Figure 4.6.

These prompts require students to consider the limits of written sources. To observe "the society in question," we show a clip from the MGM film, *The Wizard of Oz*. The clip runs from the arrival of Glinda in Munchkinland, just after Dorothy's precipitous arrival, through the discovery of the death of the Witch of the East, the celebration of the Munchkins, the arrival and departure of the Witch of the West, and the departure of Glinda in her floating bubble (Fleming, 1939). The students watch the film, which is familiar to many of them, with new eyes. As historical investigators, they look for things the film reveals that are not evident in the documents. They notice, for example, that Munchkins are little people. They observe that the Munchkins appear to maintain a standing army, since the parade for Dorothy

Figure 4.6 Second Written Sources Discussion Guide

Learning from Written Sources: Exercise I, Part 2

1. What can you learn from examining the society in question that was not evident from the written sources?
2. What does this film excerpt suggest that history is? Do you agree or disagree? What are the implications of this view of history?
3. What does this film excerpt suggest about witches?

includes uniformed soldiers carrying guns, and that the Lollipop Guild appears to have a women's counterpart, the "Lullaby League." They note that there are witches with unknown but demonstrable powers and that the power of witches seems to be geographically limited. Hecate, who was crushed by the windstorm, turns out to have been the Witch of the East, and the instrument of her death was Dorothy's house, which landed in Oz after a cyclone. The existence of the Wizard is mentioned in the film, though not in the documents. By noticing these and many other details about the film, the students begin to consider the limitations of written sources.

We then turn our attention to the question "What is history?" In the film, the Munchkins sing to Dorothy: "From now on you'll be history/ You'll be his—you'll be his—you'll be history/And we will glorify your name/You will be a bust, be a bust, be a bust/In the Hall of Fame" (Fleming, 1939). Students consider the implication of this view of history. Prior to *The Wizard of Oz* exercise, we spend a class day talking about the question "What is history" so that students can refer to their earlier discussion and compare the Munchkins' view to their own. They can talk about whether their view of history is like the Munchkins' view, or whether they think there are other important aspects to consider. They also begin to consider historical perspective. Some students point out that the story in the film is told primarily from the perspectives of the Munchkins and Glinda, who provide Dorothy with all of her information about the new land in which she finds herself. The view that the Witch of the East and the Witch of the West are evil comes from Glinda and the Munchkins, and some students ask if the story would be different if it were told from the perspective of the Witch of the West.

Since 2003, students have brought up the book and musical *Wicked*, and we have expanded the exercise to take *Wicked* into consideration. *Wicked*, a musical based on a novel by Gregory Maguire, is the back story of *The Wizard of Oz*, dealing primarily with the childhood and young adulthood of the Witch of the West and of Glinda. We distributed the lyrics to the song "Wonderful" and asked the students to consider the view of history the song suggests (Schwartz, 2003, p. 29):

> WIZARD: Elphaba, where I'm from, we believe
> all sorts of things that aren't true. We call
> it—"history."
> A man's called a traitor—or liberator
> A rich man's a thief—or philanthropist
> Is one a crusader—or ruthless invader?
> It's all in which label
> Is able to persist
> There are precious few at ease
> With moral ambiguities
> So we act as though they don't exist.

This last document gives the students a chance to think about perspective, historical judgment, and the question of revision in historical analysis. They can come up with examples of differing historical characterizations and analyses and of ideas about historical figures that have changed over time. They can think about whether an ultimate historical truth exists and how they might understand the historical events they study. Even familiar events can be reconsidered in light of differing perspectives and interpretations. This provides a good segue to the next unit in the course, which requires students to consider various views of Christopher Columbus and the historiography of contact between Europe and the Americas.

Conclusion

This exercise provides faculty with an opportunity to assess students' level of sophistication in historical analysis. More importantly, it provides students with an opportunity to assess their own views of history. Many of them have not previously considered how information gets into their history texts. Often, students begin by defining history as "facts about the past." Their encounter, as historians, with the society and the people of Oz gives them an opportunity to assess their own understanding of history and of how history is written. By the end of *The Wizard of Oz* exercise, students have had a chance to consider the ways in which historians construct analyses using documentary evidence. They have begun to consider what documents can tell them and what documents cannot reveal. They have considered the importance of prior knowledge, the importance of making historical hypotheses, and the kinds of questions documentary evidence might prompt a historian to ask. They have considered historical problems and thought about how they, as historians, might go about solving them. They have discussed questions of historical interpretation and have argued about how perspective might alter understanding of historical events. None of this requires detailed knowledge of European history. For students who have never seen the film version of *The Wizard of Oz*, and for international students, this exercise is particularly challenging. They get a real experience of beginning research on a topic about which they know nothing. For students who have seen the film, the exercise introduces historical analysis without bogging them down in preconceptions about history or in fears about their own (self-defined) inadequate knowledge.

Our experience suggests that students react well to the challenges of this assignment. They discuss the possibilities enthusiastically, and so far, although we have been working with variations on this exercise for seven years, the veteran majors and minors do not tip off the new majors and minors about the topic of the exercise. The students in the course present a wide range of paper topics with varying degrees of success. It is unusual, though, to find a student who only reports the data that he or she finds. Most of the final papers do present historical analysis rather than simple reporting. We hesitate to attribute too much about students' success or lack of success to this one exercise, but it does seem to encourage students to think analytically and to get beyond the belief that they do not know enough to create their own analyses. By using familiar, non-intimidating subject matter, we introduce students to more complex ways of thinking. *The Wizard of Oz* assessment exercise is creative in more than one sense of the word. It is creative because it uses unusual methods to solve the problem of starting a technical history course with a group of students who have different levels of historical skills. It is also creative because it encourages students to develop their own understanding of what history is and of their own potential as historical analysts. The creative assessment in which the students engage at the beginning of the course helps them to be creative historians in the later stages of the course. As the course continues, we introduce less familiar subject matter and use the skills and ideas the students developed in *The Wizard of Oz* exercise to help them develop as historians.

References

Booth, A. (2005). Worlds in collision: University tutor and student perspectives on the transition to degree level history. *Teaching History, 121,* 14–19.

Fleming, V. (Director). (1939). *The wizard of Oz* [Motion picture]. United States: Metro Goldwyn Mayer.

Hearn, M. P. (Ed.). (2000). *The annotated wizard of Oz.* New York, NY: W. W. Norton.

Michigan Department of Education. (2006). *Improving outcomes for high school students.* Retrieved May 7, 2007, from www.michigan.gov/mde/0,1607,6-140-38924---,00.html

Schwartz, S. (2003). *Wicked* [Compact disc liner notes]. New York, NY: Universal Classics Group.

Stearns, P. N. (1994). *Meaning over memory: Recasting the teaching and the culture of history.* Chapel Hill, NC: University of North Carolina Press.

5

Resurrecting the Lab Practical

Kathy Winnett-Murray

"**I** can't see anything!" is a familiar exclamation heard by biology professors. It is most often uttered by frustrated students who have peered in vain through the eyepiece of a microscope (not for the first time, but perhaps for the hundredth), earnestly searching for an elusive stoma, flagellum, or a chromosome dancing in metaphase that the text illustrations imply are "right there." Such exclamations are often accompanied by hastily sketched clusters of uniform circles residing within one big circle. Astonishingly, renditions of circles labeled stoma, flagella, and metaphase chromosomes are virtually indistinguishable from one another. The point of this exercise, of course, is to sharpen students' observational skills and to increase their competency in using an important biological tool. Come test day, however, professors typically evaluate students' ability to "see" and "do" by asking them to label the parts of a microscope (coarse focus, 40x objective, stage, eyepiece, etc.) on a two-dimensional piece of paper. The fallacy of this approach, of course, is that even if the students were able to match all mechanical parts correctly, the instructor still doesn't know very much about the students' observational skills nor their abilities to manipulate an actual microscope to find a particular structure or organism. This is not authentic assessment.

Authentic Assessment

"Authentic assessment tasks use 'real-world' and 'real-life' contexts, and are aligned with the assessment and content

56

standards in use by your institution. Students are challenged to demonstrate their achievement and skills within these domains of knowledge" (Doran, Chan, & Tamir, 1998, p. 204). The examples of authentic assessment described in this chapter are student active approaches that provide examples of how the evaluation mechanism itself (in this case, a lab practical) directly involves students, thereby encouraging them to take responsibility for their own learning. The instructor's role in carrying out such assessments involves making observations, asking questions, designing experiments, collecting and evaluating data, and reevaluating the initial questions. The assessment cycle that the instructor employs becomes directly analogous to the process that scientists themselves employ in scientific research—the scientific method (D'Avanzo, 2000).

Ironically, some forms of authentic assessment were more in vogue in the 1950s and 1960s in science laboratory courses than they appear to be now. They were called "lab practicals," they were especially common in content-rich courses such as anatomy, zoology, and botany, and they assessed precisely what the instructor wanted to know. Could the student correctly identify a particular piece of a creature—a tibia or a pistil, for example?

Program-Level Application of the Lab Practical Assessment: A Case Study

The beauty of the lab practical assessment approach is simple authenticity about what the student has learned (or not). Nonetheless, perhaps because of overall scaling back in laboratories, increasing constraints on instructor time and shared spaces at colleges and universities, lab practicals seem to have become less common, and such practical assessments of learning have been replaced by more two-dimensional tasks (e.g., filling in blanks on pictures of microscopes or on computer screens). Simultaneously, an increased emphasis on collaborative group work in lab settings, while enriching some aspects of the learning process (e.g., capitalizing on the mutual benefits that students gain when collectively employing different learning styles), has raised concerns in other aspects of learning. Most notably, how do you assure or encourage individual accountability when some or all of the work is group graded?

The individual accountability problem can be compounded in a variety of ways. Collaborative group work is not necessarily innate; it is a learned skill. The largest introductory courses are typically those that are also populated by the youngest students—the individuals who may still have a lot to learn about effective group work. Anyone who has taught introductory science labs has witnessed various manifestations of dysfunctional group work. Sometimes group work may be dominated by eager, motivated, and perhaps grade-focused personalities, and other groups may contain introverted or less motivated individuals. Some of the most inequitable distribution of tasks may occur in groups with a combination of both types, and "hiding in the group" can become a common strategy employed by some students. While it is not the intention of this chapter to discuss the role of the instructor in coaching students on how to best achieve the many benefits of effective group work, it is important to recognize that the individual accountability issue was a major impetus for my colleagues and me to develop additional means of student evaluation in laboratories that otherwise focused primarily on group work and for which most of the evaluation of student work relied on lab reports that were prepared and graded as a group effort (i.e., one lab report submitted per lab team).

In my department, we decided several years ago to remedy the ever increasing disparity between individual accountability and formats for student evaluation by resurrecting the lab practicals most of us were familiar with from our undergraduate days. We added a new twist: Instead of evaluating student learning of (solely) content-based material via lab practicals, we would create practicals in which we would directly evaluate each student's ability to *do* preselected skills that we had collectively identified as being the most important things that all biology majors should be able to do, whether that individual was a potential physician, forester, toxicologist, teacher, or genetic therapist. Thus, the practicals would include skills such as microscopy, use of various forms of instrumentation, animal handling, making serial dilutions, constructing a dichotomous key, preparing graphics with a computer program, conducting inferential statistics and hypothesis testing with computer software, and so on.

The second driving force behind the resurrection of lab practicals as a means of evaluating what students know and are able to do derived from our desire to track changes in the effectiveness of our new introductory curriculum in student learning of biological and scientific skills. Given that the make-up of particular instructors for these courses changes, in part, every semester, and given that even the content of some laboratory investigations changes from year to year, we decided that it was of utmost importance to be able to monitor the performance of students longitudinally, through time, to see how we were accomplishing these goals collectively as a department. The lab practicals have become the central assessment focus of our entire three-semester core sequence.

Now, if the stated course objective is "the student will be able to use a microscope to find, bring into focus, and identify a biological organism," instead of asking the student to label parts of a microscope on a piece of paper, an instructor or an undergraduate teaching assistant (TA) observes every student make a microscope slide preparation, place it on the microscope, successfully focus and position the creature to be viewed, and position the pointer or eyepiece micrometer on a particular part (e.g., the food vacuole of a *Paramecium*). The grader then peers into the microscope to verify that the student has located the correct structure. The instructor records, in real time, the student's ability to perform these tasks using a predetermined rubric (see Table 5.1). By using this form of authentic assessment, both the instructor and the students know if they can independently

Table 5.1 Sample Rubric for a Lab Practical

Points	Item	Notes
1	Student successfully transfers the organism	Student may attempt more than once
1	Student displays knowledge of location of light switch, coarse and fine focus, and how to position the stage	
1	Student begins with low power objective to find organism, focuses, and then uses higher power to fine focus (only)	−0.5 if student uses coarse focus on high power objective
1	Student correctly positions eyepiece pointer on a food vacuole	
1	Student turns off microscope light, aligns low power objective, and cleans stage	−1 for any item not demonstrated

use the microscope, if they can successfully manipulate the organismal target onto a slide for viewing, and if they find and "see" the correct targeted entity, for example the food vacuole, as a distinct entity in a sea of pond water (the latter would require both skill and knowledge in properly adjusting the microscope lighting, position, and focus as well as knowledge of structural relationships within the creature).

Table 5.1 shows a sample scoring rubric for a lab practical question worded as follows:

At this station you will find a compound microscope, a container of *Paramecium*, plastic pipettes, cover slips, and microscope slides. The TA will observe you as you use the pipette to transfer a *Paramecium* to a slide and prepare a wet mount for viewing. Then, using correct microscope procedures, find the Paramecium, bring it into focus at 100x magnification, and place the eyepiece pointer on the food vacuole of the organism. When you have completed this task, notify the TA, who will check the position of your pointer. The TA will then observe you as you follow correct procedures to return the *Paramecium* to the holding jar and "put away" the microscope for use by another student.

Similarly, to evaluate a student's ability to create a graph of scientific data using a computer software program, students are provided with a table of data. They are asked to enter the data into a data file then create the graphic figure. Normally, the instructor or TA then views the graph directly on the computer screen and scores various components of its accuracy using a predetermined rubric (alternatively, students can be asked to print the graph and turn it in with the practical answer sheet).

To accomplish this goal for multiple skills in our three-course introductory sequence, each of the courses was assigned certain objectives that are specifically included as part of the departmental assessment of that course (see Table 5.2, p. 69, for examples from our first and third core courses). For example, microscopy and pipetting are among the skills targeted in the first course (Cells and Genetics), surgery and use of instrumentation in the second (Organismal Biology), and field identification and use of statistical software in the third (Ecology and Evolutionary Biology). Because we intend for students to gain frequent practice with some skills, there are certain skills that are deliberately assessed more than once (e.g., hypothesis generation and testing), and some are intentionally evaluated with increasing levels of advanced application as students move through the sequential core courses (e.g., note "constructing graphs using computer" for both first and third courses in Table 5.2, p. 69). Each printed laboratory/field exercise used in our courses includes a lead section explaining the learning objectives for that lab in two categories: concepts and skills. These in turn overlap with both the stated departmental objectives and the lab practical proficiency categories that will be scored on each practical exam.

After the list of skills objectives for each introductory course was established, the group of instructors who teach a particular component of the sequence is responsible for including lab practical questions that will assess student performance on those skills. There are typically two lab practicals each semester. Each student exam contains a cover page that lists the skills that will be evaluated on that practical and a space to record information about whether the student completed that task at a proficient level. Proficiency, as defined by our department, is achieving 75% of the possible points on question tasks associated with that skill. An all-or-nothing gauge is used: the student receives a 1 for successful completion of the task, a 0 for unsuccessful completion. As instructors grade a lab practical, they simultaneously determine proficiency "1s" and "0s" for each stated skill and fill in those marks, as well as the over-all score, on each cover sheet, which is then photocopied, collated by a designated departmental assessment guru or the departmental secretary, who enters the coded 1s and 0s in a simple spreadsheet.

The inclusion of the scoring system on the exam's cover sheet also allows students to have feedback on their performance on various skills-related tasks using a list that correlates directly with the objectives that were listed for each individual lab as well as with overall objectives stated in course syllabi. Although the proficiency codes are not directly used in determination of a student's individual grade in the course, their mere presence on the cover sheet communicates to students the value that we, as a department, place on the acquisition of those skills. (Proficiency codes are correlated with the overall test score because the proficiency scores of 1 derive from the number of points received on certain questions.) Students interested in their progress over the three introductory courses are able to track their own changes in proficiency skills. And the predictable question from students—"Are these 1s and 0s part of my grade?"—provides an opportunity for the instructor to explain what we are assessing in our laboratories and, most importantly, why we are doing it. A master spreadsheet was created as an ongoing departmental database (e.g., Sundberg, 2002), which organizes every lab skill by every student. Any number of spreadsheet types could be used; we are using Microsoft Access. The spreadsheet also contains concise information about student history (e.g., advanced placement credits), first semester in a biology course at our college, and whom the student had for a lab instructor in which term. Proficiency scores (1s and 0s) are added each term and collated by a departmental assessment guru who has the task of determining the percentage of students who achieved proficiency in each skill for each semester. These results then become a part of our department's annual report to the college—thus, a permanent part of institutional record keeping.

Although unwieldy in some ways (simply by virtue of the ever increasing size of this matrix; each incoming cohort numbers about 200 students), the spreadsheet allows us to do many things. First, we can assess our own performance in meeting stated goals for each introductory course. In practice, this has been the primary use of the skills database. We have the ability to identify particular semesters, or even particular instructors for which proficiency scores are low or high on certain skills. For example, if we noted that all of the students who had Professor A were proficient in pipetting, and almost none of those who had Professor B were proficient in pipetting, we would probably ask Professor A to give Professor B a pipette tutorial before he or she teaches the course again. Such an eyebrow-raising result was evidenced for "use of taxonomic keys" in course 1 (Bio 150), fall 2001, when the percentage of proficiency scores dropped to 29% from 75%–87% recorded in the preceding years (see Table 5.2, p. 69). An example like this becomes a cause for departmental discussion (in this case, the way in which taxonomic keys were taught had changed quite a bit from the preceding years and we decided to return to the old way). On the other hand, relatively large dips and peaks across years seem to be the norm for certain skills (see "hypothesis generation and testing" in Table 5.2, p. 69), even within years. We are discovering that the proficiency scores on this skill are highly sensitive to the way in which particular practical questions are worded.

Second, we have the ability to track student progress in skills that are repeated (usually with different applications) in more than one course (e.g., note the overall improvement in "constructing graphs using computer" as students are assessed in the third biology course [Bio 280] as compared with proficiency scores in their first biology course [Bio 150] in Table 5.2) and to track longer term changes as the faculty composition and/or the nature of the student body changes from year to year. We can compare how objectives were met, or not, for different student populations (men and women, students who continue as biology majors versus those who do not, etc.).

Third, we have the ability to provide feedback to individual students who need to know how they are doing with respect to departmental goals for majors or for particular career interests. For example, students who want to go into physical therapy but have not yet demonstrated proficiency in anatomical dissection might be advised to take an elective in human or comparative anatomy where they will have ample opportunity to hone their dissection skills. Students may note that skills are assessed more than once and that their own performance may improve on a later practical for the same skill.

A significant example of how our department has made a major change in course structure as a result of assessing skills is evidenced by the skill "basic statistics using computer software." This particular skill is a manifestation of a larger student learning objective that involves the ability to analyze data that the students themselves have generated. Proficiency scores under 50% for the first three years for which we have data for the third course, along with other evidence that students struggled with analytical aspects of this course in particular, led to the creation of a required discussion section for this course in fall 2001. The discussion section focuses almost exclusively on analysis of the data for each week's lab, including the statistical analysis using computer software. Proficiency scores on this skill have improved since the implementation of the discussion section.

Benefits

Ultimately, the coordinated effort in the skills assessment has given the biology faculty a greater sense of responsibility in achieving particular outcomes deriving from our shared departmental goals and a greater sense of ownership in the introductory curriculum. A coordinated assessment endeavor that spans three courses requires a similar level of collaborative effort as that which we are expecting from our students in their group lab work. Preparation of the lab practicals is a joint effort with particular attention paid to the inclusion of sufficient and substantive questions and/or tasks for the skills proficiency assessments. When inadequate skills assessment happens, the entire group of instructors is immediately aware of it (because the same lab practical is given to all students in all lab sections), and ordinarily this is the impetus to discuss ways in which to improve our program on the next run. For institutions or individuals who are interested in exploring new ways to assess the effectiveness of individual instructors using comparative data on students who have achieved proficiency in designated skills, there is potential in using this kind of system in multiple-section courses because all instructors are implementing the same labs, the same lab practicals, and have graded the practicals in the same way. Assessing student performance on our lab practicals has also led to a greater understanding of the problems associated with measuring outcomes in other areas (e.g., content and scientific concepts), which we continue to work on developing.

Of primary importance, using lab practicals gives us confidence that we actually know what an individual student can do independently in ways that a single score on an exam does not. Being directly involved in the observation of many of our own students, one-on-one, gives us tremendous insights into the misconceptions that students have about the skills and tasks we have asked them to do.

One of the main benefits that we see, in terms of student learning processes, is that our lab practical format makes it impossible for a student's hands-on abilities to remain anonymous, as they might if lab reports were our only assessment tool. Lab practical results make us immediately aware of students who require more assistance, and more importantly, they make the student aware of it. We find that students often come to visit instructors after their first lab practical and say things like, "I really need to work on making graphs," or "I thought I knew how to operate a spectrophotometer, but I don't. Can you help me?" There are at least two positive indications in such statements: First, the skills objectives feedback has shifted student concerns, at least in part, away from "What's my grade?" and toward "What do I need to work on?" Second, it helps students pinpoint what they need to work on in ways that a single overall score on an exam cannot do as well.

Advanced students, assisting us as TAs, help in the writing of rubrics and in scoring the questions that are hands-on. Typically, TAs observe 50 or more permutations of what they thought was a simple task; TAs often remark to the instructors how surprised they are at all the different ways that students might interpret a question and carry it out. These experiences give our TAs a better understanding of their peers, and they are better poised, as a result, to help us troubleshoot while assisting in labs.

Example from an Upper Level Biology Course

Anatomy courses are traditionally the most content-rich courses one can find in the biological sciences. The sheer number of structural names of body parts to be committed to memory is overwhelming to students regardless of their level (introductory or advanced) and it is difficult to come up with successful tactics for learning mass quantities of structural terminology that work for most students. For my course, Comparative Vertebrate Anatomy (an upper level elective for biology majors), one of my stated course objectives is that "students will improve their dissection skills, their scientific writing skills, their skill at observational, descriptive analysis, and their ability to infer structure-function relationships from observations that they make through dissection." A tall order! Lab practicals are certainly not new to anatomy courses—the drawer filled with greasy specimen pins, each one flaunting a numbered bit of tape, recycled through years of anatomy lab practicals, might be a universal part of most institutions. But the approach I use for assessing this course objective on the final lab practical is to provide each student with a preserved body of a novel animal (one that they have not previously dissected in the course). During a three-hour final lab, students are asked to dissect the animal and to write their observations of the anatomy of several organ systems while they are dissecting the body. They are asked to infer, and describe in writing, the functional and structural anatomy of this animal's organ systems based on what they learned about patterns (both structural and functional) among other vertebrates over the entire semester. Thus, this exam is comprehensive in the sense that the students are expected to draw from a rich, well-developed understanding of how all vertebrate bodies are put together, in general, and also on what they have learned about the reasons for the differences when those differences exist. After writing a description (including

sketches) characterizing each organ system (e.g., repro-
ductive, cardiovascular, skeletal, digestive), students write
a summary section at the end of their essay to integrate
the structural and functional aspects of all the anatomical
systems. First, they are asked to describe what kind of a
vertebrate it is (taxonomically), to the best of their ability,
and then to write a description of the probable lifestyle
of the creature and how that lifestyle relates to the anatomy they uncovered in the past few hours. As with our
introductory courses, a major objective for the assessment
mechanism for this advanced course has been to be student active and to make the practical an important learning experience. The expectation that students will learn
new insights *while taking the exam* is integral to the students' taking responsibility for the active learning experience this provides.

Conclusion

Lab practicals, expanded from the "pinning body parts"
tradition to include evaluation of a student's competency
in performing a variety of skills, can be a valuable means
of authentic assessment because they challenge students
to actively demonstrate their achievements and skill level
at a variety of tasks and because they provide information to both instructor and student on target areas for
improvement. Skills-based lab practicals promote individual accountability for student learning, they model what is
valued in the discipline, and they can provide useful longi-
tudinal data for program improvement when a set of skills
is tracked through several years, instructors, and student
cohorts. Such practical assessment of skills is adaptable to
any other discipline in which objectives concerning "what
students are able to do" are coupled with objectives concerning "what students know."

Table 5.2 Sample Results from Biology Skills Assessment on Lab Practicals

Skill	Bio 150 F 1997	Bio 150 F 1998	Bio 150 F 1999	Bio 150 F 2000	Bio 150 F 2001	Bio 280 F 1998	Bio 280 F 1999	Bio 280 F 2000	Bio 280 F 2001	Bio 280 F 2002	Bio 280 F 2003	Bio 280 F 2004
Hypothesis generation and testing	70	—	52	40	74	65	63	97	46	72	65	83
Microscope use	—	—	34	81	35							
Use of taxonomic keys	87	75	87	—	29							
Constructing graphs using computer	60	56	45	56	63	96	73	89	95	100	92	98
Identification of biological organisms						92	58	79	95	52	55	48
Operation of instrumentation	95	50	—	—	69	—	—	—	69			
Basic statistics using computer software						41	44	45	80	59	63	62

Note. Results span several semesters. Proficiency is defined as achieving at least 75% of the points associated with questions or tasks demonstrating that skill.

References

D'Avanzo, C. (2000, July). Evaluation of course reforms: A primer on what it is and why you should do it. *Bulletin of the Ecological Society of America, 81*(3), 206–209.

Doran, R., Chan, F., & Tamir, P. (1998). *Science educator's guide to assessment.* Arlington, VA: National Science Teacher's Association.

Sundberg, M. D. (2002, Summer). Assessing student learning. *Cell Biology Education, 1*(1), 11–15.

6

Exams as Learning Experiences: One Nutty Idea After Another

Thomas Smith

The current assessment movement has its primary focus on student learning. In fact, assessment has been defined as the act or process of gathering data to better understand the strengths and weaknesses of student learning (Harris & Hodges, 1995). In particular, classroom assessment has been defined as an approach designed to help teachers find out what students are learning in the classroom and how well they are learning it (Angelo & Cross, 1993). On the other hand, noted leaders in the field continue to recognize that "students have a tendency to learn what teachers *inspect* rather than what they *expect*" (Angelo & Cross, 1988, p. 156; emphasis added).

Therefore, in light of this focus on student learning and in recognition of the motivation that is often behind student learning, several long-standing student evaluation (inspection) methods may require a fresh approach. The preparation, administration, and grading of objective classroom exams is one such method. For our purposes, objective classroom exams will be classified as those exams that are made up of a series of questions that allow students to demonstrate both the knowledge they have acquired and their ability to process and use that knowledge (Palomba & Banta, 1999). Thus, the overriding objective for this assessment approach will be to utilize the entire process, from preparation through grading, of an objective classroom exam and transform it or manage it in ways that provide insight into the accomplishment of the primary learning objectives for the class. In other words, how can we take what has essentially been a significant performance evaluation process on students and turn it into primarily an assessment tool, one that can be used as a significant learning opportunity for the instructor?

The setting used to implement this approach is a junior-level financial management class. The study and practice of financial management primarily tries to address two basic questions: 1) What investments should we make with the cash we have? and 2) Where should the cash come from in the first place? (Brigham & Houston, 2004). This requires knowledge of financial vocabulary, terms, and equations, but of greater importance is the need for acute analytical reasoning. As such, the primary learning objectives for the student involve improving his or her skills at analyzing information, questions, or problems to understand them more fully and solve them more effectively. These analytical and critical thinking skills are examples of procedural learning—learning the "how" rather than the "what" (Angelo & Cross, 1993). The assessment approach taken with an objective classroom exam is by no means exclusive to this class; in fact, it is quite easily transferable to other classes and courses with similar learning objectives.

Tactics to Complement the Traditional Classroom Exam

Five tactical strategies are utilized in moving the classroom examination process away from evaluation and more toward an assessment of student-learning outcomes. These strategies will be discussed in greater detail and include 1) providing students with access to exams from previous semesters, 2) conducting review sessions, 3) allowing students the use of a cheat sheet during the exam, 4) preparing exam questions that require a justification with the answer, and 5) individually grading each exam with the student. Even though the grading of each exam with the student is perhaps the most controversial and unusual tactic, it must be stressed that it is the combination of all five tactics that provide the stimulus necessary to break the evaluation-only perceptions attached to traditional objective classroom exams. The remainder of this chapter will be broken down into six sections. The first five sections will describe each of the five tactical strategies, including how each on its own has helped to shed light on the achievement of the primary learning objectives. The final section will highlight some of the additional systemic effects and benefits of these five tactical strategies and will underscore how they transform the traditional objective classroom exam into a highly useful and powerful assessment tool.

Access to Previous Exams

Several weeks prior to an exam, copies of exams given in previous semesters are placed on reserve in the library. Exams from the past two semesters are adequate. Only the questions are placed on reserve, not the answers. If students want to know the correct answers, they will have to see the instructor in person or come to the review session. In this manner, the procedure and thinking process required to derive the correct answer can be discussed and emphasized as opposed to students simply seeing if their answer matches the correct one. Thus, the observation and inquiry into the students' level of understanding of the primary learning objectives can begin with the process of preparing for the exam.

The initial motivation for providing access to previous exams stemmed from an observation that fraternity and sorority members had access to exams from previous semesters. This did not seem fair to the non-Greek students, so I decided to make the exams available to all students. Not only did this level the playing field, but it seemed to elevate the level of performance and learning for everyone. This was a classic example of the law of unintended consequences, except that the consequences in this case happened to be quite positive.

There were several other positive consequences that resulted from this move. First, it relieved much of the stress and anxiety that students have regarding format, style, and the overall difficulty level of exam questions. Second, it proved to be a wonderful tool to guide student questions during review sessions (to be discussed in a later section) and outside of class. Finally, knowing that copies of all the old exams over the past years would be in the hands of every student in the class created an additional burden of having to write new exam questions for every exam during every semester. Although writing new exam questions is not necessarily a positive, it forced me to be up-to-date and fresh with every exam question.

Conducting Review Sessions

Review sessions are scheduled on the evening before the exam is to be given. These sessions usually last about two hours and students are free to come and go at their leisure. Students generally come to these sessions having already studied much of the material. For most of them, these review sessions hold a two-fold purpose. First, it is a "just in case" exercise to see if there are any major content gaps in their studying thus far. Second, it is a chance to check their answers on the previous semester's exams.

The review session provides a wonderful teaching opportunity in that students are very attentive. In other words, it is a prime learning opportunity. The structure of the sessions is question and answer. Almost all of the student questions originate from questions on the previous exams. They begin by asking what the correct answer is to a certain exam question. After the answer is provided, a second related question will usually follow. This question will take the form, "How did you get that answer?" Instead of immediately mapping out the thinking process that led to the answer, I like to push back and ask students how they would attack the problem. Once again, this process is of tremendous benefit because it provides a window into the level of sophistication in the students' thinking processes. Once the topic has been exhausted, another student will ask for the answer to a different test question and the process will repeat.

The idea of scheduling review sessions and using previous exams to review classroom material is another example of how the outcomes from a strategic tactic generated several additional positive and unintended consequences. First, when the previous exams were made available to students, they simply based their questions on these exams. This allowed for the review sessions to focus on the most significant material. Second, students described how the review session, in particular the timing of the session, became the key to how they managed their study time. They described the review session as the "centerpiece" for their study strategy. Finally, even though attendance at these sessions was voluntary, a vast majority (80%–90%) of students took advantage of the opportunity. Because the review took place outside the formality of the classroom, it was much more conducive to open dialogue. Students who never spoke in class would liven up at the review session. The downside consequence, though not unintended, is the use of additional instructor time during the evening. Given the nature and extent of the learning that occurs in these review sessions, I suggest that the review session substitute for regular class time if the instructor is extremely pressed for time.

Use of a Cheat Sheet During the Exam

Each student is allowed to bring a cheat sheet into the exam. The sheet is limited to a certain size (a 5 x 7 index card worked for my purposes) and must be handwritten. There is no limitation on the material that can be written on the sheet. Students are also provided with a basic calculator at the time of the exam. The content on each student's cheat sheet does not vary too much. It is primarily composed of definitions, formulas, and step-by-step instructions on how to solve certain types of problems. The source of this material comes from the textbook, class notes, and the discussion at the review session.

The basic intent of allowing the use of a cheat sheet is to send the proper signals to the student. Students realize that they don't need to, and should not, memorize the material. Any fact or formula that they feel compelled to memorize can simply be written on their index card. Furthermore, it reemphasizes to the student that the primary learning objective is process oriented and not memorization of content. The cheat sheet acts in a similar fashion to the first two tactics in that it allows students to focus most of their attention on the primary learning objective.

When students knew at the beginning of the semester that they would have access to a cheat sheet for the exam, it actually altered the way they studied and managed the course material. Throughout the semester, they would approach their various assignments and projects with an eye toward understanding and appreciating the various factors, tradeoffs, and cause and effect relationships inherent in financial management decision-making. This was in marked contrast to the traditional approach of simply searching for right answers. The preparation of the cheat sheet provided students with a method to structure the course material and organize their thoughts. For some students, this was the first time they had ever used this method as part of their test-taking strategy. Thus, it provided them with a new skill that could be used for the current exam as well as other classes.

One of the most gratifying unforeseen consequences from the use of a cheat sheet was the stress-relieving effect it had on students. The combined tactics of having access to previous exams and allowing a cheat sheet seemed to relieve most of the natural anxiety associated with the taking of any exam. Finally, of great interest was that almost none of the students actually referred to their cheat sheet while taking the exam. If they did, it was used as a double check, much like a calculator is used to double-check simple mathematical calculations. It appears that material was committed to memory, at least short term, when the students had organized their thoughts and written them down in a structured manner.

Exam Questions that Require an Answer with a Justification

The exams for this course consist of 25 to 30 items; the exam is administered during a one hour and twenty minute class period. Each exam question takes the form of an "enhanced" multiple choice. There are generally five options, and when appropriate, two of these choices include "all of the above" and "none of the above." The enhancement to the traditional multiple choice question is that students must provide a written justification for the choice they circled. When it comes to grading the exam, the written justification is what is evaluated, not the specific choice that is circled. Thus, students may receive partial or no credit if they circled the correct choice yet provided an inadequate or incorrect justification. On the other hand, students may receive full or partial credit if they circled the incorrect choice yet provided a reasonable alternative justification or utilized a set of different reasonable working assumptions. See Figure 6.1 for three simple examples that demonstrate this type of question.

The suitability and appropriateness of the exam questions are based on how well they are able to assess the achievement of the primary learning objectives. It is imperative to spend ample time on writing suitable and appropriate exam questions because not only do these questions set up the type of discussion that will be generated during the grading process (see below), but they also lay the groundwork for the primary study content and the focus of review sessions that will occur in the near future. Thus, each exam question has both present and future implications.

Individually Grading Each Exam with the Student

After the exam has been completed, each student must arrange for an individual appointment with the instructor. The appointment is set for 15 minutes with the goal of completing all appointments one week after the exam is

Figure 6.1 Sample Exam Questions Illustrating How Students Must Justify Answers

1. For the year 2006, what will be the immediate result(s) of Bath Industries' decision to issue $8 million in *stocks*? Base your answer on this decision alone. **You must explain your answer to receive credit.** (4)

   a. Bath Industries' earnings per share (EPS) *will* decrease.
   b. Bath Industries' total assets *will* decrease.
   c. Bath Industries' total liabilities *will* decrease.
   d. All of the above.
   e. None of the above.

2. For the year 2006, what will be the immediate result(s) of Bath Industries' decision to borrow $15 million through a long-term loan (bonds)? Base your answer on this decision alone. **You must explain your answer to receive credit.** (4)

   a. Bath Industries' total liabilities *will* increase.
   b. Bath Industries' cash *will* increase.
   c. Bath Industries' overall riskiness *will* increase.
   d. All of the above.
   e. None of the above.

3. Recall that the equation for the Security Market Line (SML) is as follows: $k_i = k_{RF} + (k_M - k_{RF})\, b_i$

   Assume the required rate of return on a one-year U.S. Treasury bond is 5.0% and the required rate of return on the market portfolio is 11.5%. Also, assume the *expected* rate of return for Bath Industries is 13.0% and the beta for Bath is 1.20.

   Now, also assume the federal government is successful in implementing massive tax cuts for both individuals and corporations. How will this new governmental policy affect the default risk premium on Bath Industries' bonds? **You must explain your answer to receive credit.** (3)

   a. The default risk premium on Bath Industries' bonds will increase.
   b. The default risk premium on Bath Industries' bonds will decrease.
   c. The new governmental policy will have no effect on the default risk premium on Bath Industries' bonds.

administered. Exams are not graded until students show up at their prearranged time. The primary purpose of the appointment is to systematically discuss each exam question and its corresponding answer. The focus of this discussion is on the student's justification of his or her circled choice. It is at this time that the amount of credit to be received for each answer is determined.

The actual process of grading the exam occurs at a table where the instructor and student sit side by side with the student's ungraded exam placed between them. The instructor begins to read the exam, item by item, together with the student. After each answer, one of three things happens. First, a quick discussion and determination of credit occurs when the student has provided the correct circled choice and an adequate and thorough justification. It is clearly evident that the student understands the thinking process required for this particular scenario. In this situation, because time is limited, a few words of encouragement and compliment must suffice.

Second, a fairly quick and somewhat more difficult discussion occurs when the student has provided the correct or incorrect circled choice but has not provided a proper or reasonable justification. As in the first case, the determination of credit is quick and easy because it is clearly evident that the student does not grasp the concept or the required thinking process. To begin the discussion for this particular situation, I make the following straightforward request that takes the general form of "Describe your thinking process when trying to answer this question." When this request is on the table, most students quickly confess that they do not understand the concept or the required thinking process. In any case, the discussion must soon be directed toward providing the information, knowledge, and/or skills necessary to bring the student up to the appropriate level of understanding or to correct his or her misunderstanding. The length of time devoted to this discussion will depend on the degree of understanding. Students with little to no understanding are advised to set up a time with the instructor at a later date.

The final situation occurs when the student has provided an incorrect circled choice with a justification that has some redeeming value or when the student has provided the correct circled choice with a less than adequate or thorough justification. Unlike the first two situations, I try to spend as much of the allotted time discussing the student's thought processes on these particular questions as needed. This is precisely the situation in which critical, and often hidden, information can be gleaned to improve the teaching process to ultimately improve the learning process. Therefore, much care is taken in listening to the various assumptions, cause and effect relationships, and analytical reasoning that were used in arriving at a particular answer. An analogy can be drawn from the Total Quality Management movement in its early years of implementation in Japan. Although producing products with minor defects was not the objective, a product that was discovered with a new or unique defect was cause for celebration. This was because the ultimate discovery of the root cause of the problem inevitably led to a positive and long-lasting change in the production process. Furthermore, until the specific defect was produced and detected, the flaw in the manufacturing process remained unknown (Deming, 1986). Now, the point here is not to celebrate when a minor defect is detected in a student's answer but to treat it as a wonderful opportunity and gather as much information as possible.These are prime teachable moments for both the student and the instructor.

An interesting phenomenon occurs after the first day of appointments. The correct answers and reasonable approaches to reaching these answers spread to the rest of the students. Whereas students on the first day are somewhat anxious, nervous, and tentative, many students now arrive at their appointment armed with newfound knowledge and confidence. They also arrive with an understanding of where and how they "messed up." The primary objectives of the discussions remains the same—increasing students' level of understanding and ability and assessing where the teaching methodology may be improved, but the determination of credit becomes a bit more difficult. Students are now able to verbally provide a reasonable justification for their circled choices in spite of what their written justification may indicate. This is a minor inconvenience in light of the fact that students are now teaching other students what they have learned, raising the learning outcomes for all involved.

As one can imagine, this is a significant time commitment on the part of the instructor. As with the review session, I recommend that one class session during the week be devoted to these appointments. Because one class period was usually devoted to going over the exam with the entire class anyway, this cancellation does not cut into precious class time. But there is no magical way of getting around the significant amount of time that must be devoted to this tactic. With approximately 25 students in each of two sections, and roughly 15 minutes per appointment, the time commitment would entail 12 to 13 hours. The class would meet on a Tuesday and Thursday schedule. An exam would be given on Tuesday, and by the next Tuesday, all 50 appointments would be complete and we would be ready to grapple with new material.

Systemic Effects and Benefits from All Five Tactical Strategies

As mentioned earlier, it is important to realize that the benefits that accrue from transforming the objective classroom exam into an assessment tool are best understood in the context of all five strategies acting together. Each strategy is a cog in a larger system, and there are many interdependencies among the various tactics. For example, the exams from previous semesters generate and focus discussion at the review session and provide guidance for information that will be useful on a cheat sheet, and objective exam questions that require a justification facilitate the appropriate discussion during the grading process as well as becoming the content for the exams that will be pored over by next semester's students.

The first noticeable systemic effect is that students are willing to work harder. The motivation for this has both extrinsic and intrinsic roots. There is a lot more accountability throughout the entire examination process. While students do not want to embarrass themselves while their exam is being graded, they are quite proud and eager to discuss questions in which they are able to think through a scenario and come up with the "best" answer. For many students, the entire process proves difficult and joyful at the same time. When asked, students respond that the enjoyment is primarily the result of seeing the connection and consistency between the procedural learning goal of the class and the classroom exam. The openness on the part of the student facilitates the use of these discussions as a tool for teaching improvements.

The second effect goes along with the frankness and sincerity displayed by students. The entire process helps to build a trusting relationship between the student and the instructor. Students are much more comfortable asking questions in the classroom and dropping by the office on an informal basis. The nature of the questions that students ask also changes. The all too typical "Will this be on the exam?" question is replaced by "How would you go about solving a problem of this sort?" Class time is simply less formal and guided more by students' inquisitiveness than by the instructor's lecture.

The information gleaned from transforming the classroom exam into an assessment tool led to a transformation in the teaching pedagogy used in the financial management class. It has become clear that a pedagogy that utilizes the case study approach is conducive to developing students' ability to think through financial problems and situations. In particular, an ideal case study replicates the complex and ambiguous situations that one encounters in the field of finance.

Students are given ample opportunity to prepare themselves to do well on the exam through the process of providing access to previous exams, offering and conducting a review session, and allowing the use of a cheat sheet. The instructor is afforded the opportunity to truly assess student learning on key procedural learning objectives by writing exam questions that require student justification and then grading each exam with the individual student. In other words, even though the classroom exam can still maintain its traditional evaluative function, utilizing these five tactical strategies in conjunction with the objective classroom exam can transform the entire process into an extremely useful assessment instrument.

References

Angelo, T. A., & Cross, K. P. (1988). *Classroom assessment techniques: A handbook for faculty.* San Francisco, CA: Jossey-Bass.

Angelo, T. A., & Cross, K. P. (1993). *Classroom assessment techniques: A handbook for college teachers* (2nd ed.). San Francisco, CA: Jossey-Bass.

Brigham, E. F., & Houston, J. F. (2004). *Fundamentals of financial management, concise edition* (4th ed.). Mason, OH: Thompson South-Western.

Deming, W. E. (1986). *Out of the crisis.* Cambridge, MA: Massachusetts Institute of Technology, Center for Advanced Educational Services.

Harris, T. L., & Hodges, R. E. (Eds.). (1995). *The literacy dictionary: The vocabulary of reading and writing.* Newark, DE: International Reading Association.

Palomba, C. A., & Banta, T. W. (1999). *Assessment essentials: Planning, implementing, and improving assessment in higher education.* San Francisco, CA: Jossey-Bass.

7

Web-Based Instruction and Assessment in a German Culture Course

Lee Forester

The Contemporary German Culture course has been a staple in college and university German departments for decades. Typically it targets students in their junior year, addresses both high culture and low culture, and offers an introduction to political, legal, and other institutions in Germany. Students are encouraged to analyze German cultural phenomena from a more informed and distanced viewpoint. Assessments typically include quizzes, tests, and a final paper or project.

While the need for cultural understanding is indeed urgent, advanced language students in these culture courses often sense a disconnect between their classroom-based learning and the very real tasks they face in using German outside the classroom. Many will study or do an internship in a German-speaking country. Yet traditional classroom teaching in a culture course—and especially assessments such as quizzes, tests, and papers—usually does not meet these students' actual linguistics needs. Such courses can quickly become "facts about Germany" rather than actual cross-cultural encounters that prepare students for life outside the university.

With this disconnect in mind, I decided in 1997 to create a new German culture course, Germany Live, with the goal of bringing the students as much as possible into direct contact with German culture, both institutions and modes of everyday life. To achieve this, I felt that the World Wide Web should play a major role both for student learning (using German web sites for cultural and linguistic information) as well as student production and assessment. It was hoped that using the web would make the connection to German culture more direct because sites would be current, unlike books published many years before. In addition, students were already showing signs of considering the web to be "truer" than library books. Students began to quote web pages as sources of information in their papers and showed increasing lack of interest in books. I hoped that using a number of German-language web sites would seem more relevant and that students would take their learning more seriously because of this. To date, I have taught this redesigned course four times.

Rather than assigning readings from books or newspaper articles that would form the basis of classroom lecture or discussion, I decided to approach German culture based on approximately 20 different topics, such as nature, the automobile, the sea, war, east-west relations, and the like. Traditional reading assignments would still play a role, but a large part of student preparation for class would involve web searches based on concepts and vocabulary relevant to the topics of the week. Students would have worksheets with 15 terms that they would have to research on their own using the web before and during class. This would give students an opportunity to improve their research skills and ability to analyze and assess information on the web. And because there was no single canonical source for "correct" answers, students could help each other form a fuller idea and understanding of each topic.

As a logical extension of a web-based approach to reading, I decided to forego traditional papers or essays and instead require students to submit all of their work as web sites. Each student would create and maintain a course web site and post all homework and larger projects there. This would give the students concrete experience in web site creation, a skill that would probably be useful whatever their final occupation after college. It also made all of their work public because anyone could come to their web site and view the pages they created. I discovered right away that students took their work much more seriously because of this, knowing that the whole world was watching. Their work was thus not a private exchange between them and their instructor; it was a public contribution and, for their later projects, an attempt to contribute to the web itself. Matters such as accuracy of facts, grammatical correctness, and vocabulary usage seemed much more important when others besides the instructor had access to their work.

The Course

The 15-week course met three times a week for an hour in a closed computer lab and was organized into three distinct phases. The first three weeks of the course were devoted to training students to produce reasonable web pages and web sites from a technical and a design point of view. This included an introduction to an HTML editor such as Dreamweaver as well as instruction in creating and editing digital images, either from scans, digital photographs, or other digital sources. In addition, students were instructed in basic HTML itself so that they could edit HTML files without using an editor and in using file transfer protocol (FTP) to transfer files from a local computer to their college server account. Some discussion was dedicated to issues of copyright, both for images and for referencing other web pages and text. Nearly all of this preliminary instruction took place in German so that students became familiar with German terminology relevant to computers and the Internet. Class time was divided into two parts. During the first 15 to 20 minutes I presented material verbally using computer projections to illustrate the principles. Students spent the rest of each hour working on small projects, either alone or in small groups, while I tutored individuals and groups as needed. During this three-week period, students first produced several small web pages. Their culminating project was a personal home page (in German), which they uploaded to accounts that the college provided to them on the college web server and that could be accessed by anyone, anywhere. Students considered their classmates (and family and friends) to be their primary audience, but there was also a larger audience out there on the Internet.

The next phase consisted of 10 weeks of content. Rather than focusing on facts about Germany (dates, institutions, economic statistics), students worked with several themes in contemporary Germany, using select readings and, in later courses, videos associated with the German television series *Hundert Deutsche Jahre* (100 German Years), which was produced just before 2000. Each of the 52 episodes from this series addresses a specific topic (e.g., "The Sea," "The Automobile," "Elections") from a cultural and historical point of view, connecting it to various points during the years 1900–2000. Because the materials were produced by Germans for Germans, they offered an exceptional opportunity to explore German self-identity and contrast it to North American perspectives. Each week students wrote reviews of their reading and posted them to their web site, and they completed a mini-research web site on some aspect of the material covered in the videos. For example, during the week when "Das Auto" was viewed, students designed web sites on Porsche, BMW, differences in German driver training, and the like. Students were able to choose their own mini-topics to help make the assignment personal and relevant (see Figures 7.1 and 7.2 for samples of student work). One class period a week was spent viewing and discussing one of the episodes of *Hundert Deutsche Jahre*, while the other two class periods were spent working on their projects, individually and in small groups, helping each other and receiving assistance and guidance from me as needed.

Students spent the last two weeks of the semester working on and presenting final projects: more extensive web sites exploring topics in German culture addressed in the course. While some students elected to work on their own,

Figure 7.1 Sample Student Web Page from "Das Auto"
Assignment

most students chose to work in groups of two or three. Like their other coursework, all student projects were posted to the course web site and were available to the world. Students demonstrated and explained their web sites to the class during the last few days of instruction. My evaluation of their coursework was based on their many small web projects, summaries of reading and video viewing, participation, and their final web project.

Figure 7.2 Sample Student Web Page on "Ostalgie"

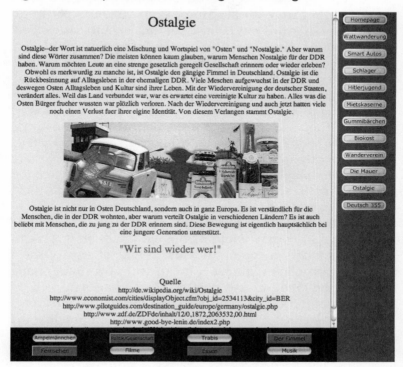

The Effects of Change

With the focus on group-based web site production as the final product, the nature of this culture course changed substantially from previous versions. On one hand, the course required a great deal more time to set up. Bringing in appropriate, useful web sites, designing web-based learning tasks, and assuring a somewhat comprehensive survey of key German cultural themes, icons, and practices required much more preparation up front. In addition, adding web-based production skills to content goals required students to invest more time in the course than they had in the past.

One of the first surveys of students after five weeks indicated that they were working more than 15 hours per week on homework for this one course, an unacceptable workload in their minds. Yet the nature of the work (designing web pages, searching for and assimilating information on the web) seemed to be less odious to them than more traditional learning tasks in language courses, and thus most students were willing to spend considerably more time than usually would be the case. Student perception of time and work can be vastly different between print and computer media. It seems partly to do with a belief that creative work on a computer is "play" rather than work. It was not unusual for some groups to spend many hours a day working on their final project and yet not consider it to be a burden.

It also became clear during this redesigned course that, with regard to course content, the old adage that "less is more" was true. To equip students to take charge of their own web portfolios required a great deal of training, both in the actual creation and posting of web pages as well as in overall matters of tasteful web design and organization. The first 3 weeks of the course concentrated on building up the skills and tools to help students succeed in the remaining 12 weeks. While at times I bristled at this perceived loss of time in content, in the end the results were far more impressive than in a traditional course because of students' increased ownership and willingness to work hard.

My role as an instructor changed from the classic "sage on the stage" to the "guide on the side." Although I had hoped this would happen, when it actually did, the effect was at times disconcerting. During many class periods, as students worked in small groups, my role was to help with design issues, technical questions, and other forms of individualized guidance. Some days this might involve me explaining how to create frames in a web page and why one might wish to and why one might not wish to. Other times I served as a linguistic consultant and helped them with their language, though I did not choose to correct everything they posted. Often I helped groups by giving them hints or suggestions on where they might search for information they were seeking. This kind of teaching was pleasing at the moment, but it forced me to rethink my role and especially how to keep content learning relatively uniform while also allowing a great deal of latitude for student independence. Because I was no longer the conduit of all information, leading class became an exercise in supervising independent learners. Because the class met in a computer lab, it was easy to have the groups work together and stay abreast of what other groups were doing and intervene from time to time. This also had the benefit of allowing me to get to know the students better and to develop a rapport that is often missing in a traditional lecture-based course.

One of the greatest benefits I observed was the number of times small groups, completely engrossed in their task, communicated in German. It was quite satisfying to hear them using German without consciously reflecting on their decision to do so. That is, their German became automatic and occurred in a natural setting. Often it seems that this authentic and natural language use can only happen in countries where the target language is spoken, but the design of this course proved that there can be environments in the speakers' native countries where authentic second language use can both occur and thrive. This was excellent preparation for study abroad.

Changes in student behaviors in this course were also evident. Virtually all students exhibited much more ownership of their assignments because they were available for the world to see. Nearly all students requested assistance with spelling, formatting, and content where previously they might have been satisfied just to turn in something with errors. It quickly became obvious that many were emailing the links to their work to their parents, friends, and roommates. And because many of the topics were close to their own interests, students showed a great deal more interest in the content of their own work. Since virtually all of their research was performed online, it seemed less onerous to them than traditional library research, and consequently many spent much more time on the task than might have otherwise been the case.

Through comparing their own writing with the sources they were reading on German language web sites, students quickly became aware of the deficiencies in their own German. Class time was devoted to the tricky question of copying language patterns observed on the web. On one hand, appropriating authentic language structures, word choice, phrases, and syntax is an excellent way to become more proficient in a foreign language. But it also became apparent that the class needed to clarify the line between inspiration and plagiarizing. It is extremely easy to cut and copy a few sentences into a web site. Yet this did not further the goal of increased language learning. Thus, part of several class sessions were spent discussing how to identify interesting and useful linguistic structures in German and then appropriate them in one's own writing without plagiarizing actual content.

Results

A few anecdotes will illustrate highlights and moments when this course redesign led to unexpected results or at least to results quite a bit different than are usually achieved in a traditional book-based culture course.

Several class assignments involved students studying a current issue in Germany such as environmental protection, demonstrations against new airport construction, imposing speed limits on the Autobahn, and similar topics. Because the student web sites were available to the world, a number of Germans stumbled upon our student pages while surfing. We received several emails from Germans who were both surprised and pleased to find American students learning German and actually addressing real topics. A few Germans wrote that they wished they had been able to learn English the same way these students were learning

German. To have their work validated by German speakers was both exciting and satisfying to the students.

An Austrian exchange student was enrolled in one course. Normally a standard culture course would have been a complete waste of time for a native speaker, but because developing web skills was a key goal, the student learned a great deal. The cultural comparison between Europe and North America was also revealing. It was an unexpected benefit to have a course where both native and nonnative speakers could participate and learn equally. Even more fulfilling was the note this exchange student sent after returning home: Using his new HTML skills, he had secured a job as a webmaster at an Austrian company and expressed his gratitude for the real skills he had gained in the course.

One small group chose as their project a cross-cultural survey about attitudes toward friendship, authority, romantic relationships, work, and travel. This was to be conducted with their American friends as well as with Germans. The group was responsible for contacting Germans whom they did not know and encouraging them to complete the online survey and discuss it with them. Naturally this all had to happen in German, and the American students were quite nervous about posting to German-language newsgroups looking for participants. But they overcame their fears and recruited a large number of informants, and the resulting survey and analysis of the results were interesting not only to the course participants but also to the Germans who participated. In a way, it was a very basic precursor to the well-known Cultura project (Furstenberg, Levet, English, & Maillet, 2001). The small group that created this project felt pride in their accomplishment and also worked through their nervousness in dealing with native German speakers.

In the first offering of this course, one student did a final project on German hip-hop. Because I encouraged students to initiate direct contacts with Germans, she emailed several German hip-hop bands and asked questions about hip-hop. This led not only to a very informed and accurate web site on German hip-hop but also to transatlan-tic friendships: When the student traveled to Germany to study for two years, she met several of the hip-hop artists she had contacted by email, making her learning in that course very relevant and very real.

Conclusion

Certainly not every student had a Cinderella story or showed a complete personal transformation or paradigm shift in this new course, but it was clear that the decision to use web sites as the venue for student linguistic output and assessment was more than justified by the positive results. This course continues to have the highest enrollments of all upper division German courses at my institution, and the benefits of heightening student interest, improving linguistic ability, and preparing students for overseas study have been clear. Naturally, a course that is based in new media will never be the same twice, and adjustments to new communication technologies must continually take place. The next time the course is offered it will include blogs, podcasts, and other media as they become available and popularly accepted. The benefits of direct contact with German speakers, the development of real-world skills in communication and creation of web content, the high degree of personal ownership of their work, and the natural second language communication in class are benefits that more than justify the extra work required to set up such a course.

References

Bähr, G. A. (Producer). (1998–1999). *Hundert deutsche Jahre* [Television series]. Germany: SWR.

Furstenberg, G., Levet, S., English, K., & Maillet, K. (2001, January). Giving a virtual voice to the silent language of culture: The Cultura project. *Language Learning and Technology, 5*(1), 55–102.

8

Challenging Students (and the Professor) to Use All of Their Brains: A Semester-Long Exercise in Thinking Styles and Synthesis

Elizabeth A. Trembley

Aha! That wonderful moment when a student "gets" course material in a way that surpasses knowledge. When suddenly the student understands *herself* afresh within the context of new skills and information.

Her face lights up. Her shoulders hunch a little closer to the book. Her finger traces a certain line of text for a neighbor. They may even share a smile.

All because somehow this student has connected her new learning to her understanding of herself and the world.

The semester-long project described in this chapter does many things, but most exciting among them is the amount of ownership and enthusiasm it generates among students. This arises primarily from the development of skills in the context of the Herrmann Brain Dominance Instrument™, a thinking styles preference assessment. This assessment helps students understand themselves and their modes of thinking in clear ways, providing them with a new model and a new language for discussing what they previously conceived of as merely personal preference. With this as a foundation, students spend a semester learning how they and others communicate, then develop web pages exploring contemporary critical issues in ways that appeal to and educate the broadest possible audience. Over and over during the several phases of this project, three skills are built and reinforced: understanding multiple ways of thinking;

thinking critically about fact, proof, and bias; and increasing computing competence.

To help students build these skills, I use a work-assessment-feedback-work loop throughout the semester as each phase of the project rolls into the next. I have found this to be a successful design for assessing the learning, transfer, synthesis, and application of three initially unrelated skills. This continuous loop of assessment allows me to adjust instruction as needed.

Though I use certain specific skills for my development of this semester-long assessment tool, I believe the overall design—teaching three specific skills and developing a complex, multilayered project that synthesizes the use of all three—would work with virtually any three skills assuming they reflect different cognitive abilities and combine into a meaningful project. So, while this example refers to the specifics of my course, none of those is essential to the success of this assessment design.

Overview

In brief, the project looks like this. First, students dive into the development of three new skills:

- Understanding and practicing multiple ways of thinking, including specific modes which they do not naturally prefer
- Thinking critically about fact, proof, and bias—in particular exploring how different people with different mental preferences value very different kinds of "information" as "fact" or "proof" or "bias"
- Increasing computing competence using Dreamweaver to design web pages, Excel to graphically represent statistics, and various types of image modification software to prepare images for use in web pages

The experiences for discovering and practicing these skills take approximately one-third of the semester, or five weeks.

Second, students begin work on the project that fills the rest of the term: Each creates web pages that explore a contemporary critical issue. They may select any topic of interest to them. They know from the start that their work will be published to the college community at the conclusion of the semester. However, I do not give this assignment to students as one big project. Though they understand the big picture, they move through the stages of development one at a time. Each portion of the web project is drafted and assessed by small peer groups and by me. Students receive feedback from this assessment and use it to revise that portion of their project and improve on the next portion, which goes through the same work-assessment-feedback-work loop.

Finally, students submit their polished web pages on CD-ROM. I publish them on a class web site open to the college. In whole class workshops, students present their final work to the rest of the class for assessment and feedback, and I provide written evaluation of the overall web products.

As students work through each step of the project, their performance is evaluated in terms of the three basic skills. Using "primary trait analysis" as defined by Walvoord and McCarthy (1990), my students and I together use the basic act of recording grades as an assessment device. In particular, we attend to "performance strengths and weaknesses in individual pieces" of the overall, semester-long assignment. Each skill is closely related to the other and each is assessed—by me and by the small peer groups—multiple times in the course. This basic construct of classroom assessment, Angelo's (1991) "early and often," helps students "improve their learning strategies and study habits in order to become more independent, successful learners" (p. 17). In addition, these frequent direct measures of performance enable me to evaluate students' command of the skills and adjust subsequent instruction as needed to help them achieve strong results at the end of the term.

Pre-Project Preparation

The first step in the project is the preparatory work done in the first five weeks of the semester. This not only introduces students to the skills I will later assess (understanding multiple ways of thinking; thinking critically about fact, proof, and bias; and increasing computing competence), but it also provides them with models and low or no point opportunities to practice and receive feedback before having to apply the skills to the web page project.

As soon as the course begins, students take the Herrmann Brain Dominance Instrument™ (HBDI), a thinking styles inventory, to begin their development of the first skill: understanding multiple ways of thinking. This assessment works from the Whole Brain Model™ (see Figure 8.1) that identifies four distinct modes of knowing:

- A quadrant: A thinker preferring this mode "favors activities that involve analyzing, dissecting, figuring out, solving problems logically, and getting facts" (Herrmann, 1995, p. 79).
- B quadrant: Thinkers preferring this mode, like those preferring the A quadrant, are verbal with a "linear approach" that rejects ambiguity and tends toward controlling. This thinking mode focuses on what has worked in the past, tackles one thing at a time, perfects detail, and keeps things safe and predictable (Herrmann, 1995, pp. 80–81).
- C quadrant: "Sensitive and receptive," this quadrant focuses on "mood, atmospheres, attitudes, and energy levels," develops a kinesthetic relationship with experience, values emotion, spirituality, and human processes. This mode tends to expand possibilities (Herrmann, 1995, pp. 82–83).
- D quadrant: This mode brings originality and risk-taking, a devotion to "new ideas, possibilities, variety, oddities, incongruities, and questions that sound obvious

Figure 8.1 Whole Brain Model

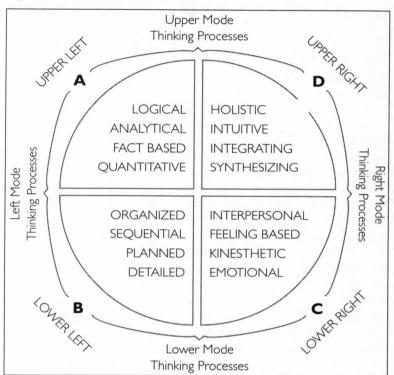

Upper Mode
Thinking Processes

UPPER LEFT

A

UPPER RIGHT

D

LOGICAL
ANALYTICAL
FACT BASED
QUANTITATIVE

HOLISTIC
INTUITIVE
INTEGRATING
SYNTHESIZING

Left Mode
Thinking Processes

Right Mode
Thinking Processes

ORGANIZED
SEQUENTIAL
PLANNED
DETAILED

INTERPERSONAL
FEELING BASED
KINESTHETIC
EMOTIONAL

LOWER LEFT

B

LOWER RIGHT

C

Lower Mode
Thinking Processes

but actually go to the heart of the matter" (Herrmann, 1995, p. 84).

The model also links these modes to their nearest neighbors (the upper and lower mode processes and the left and right mode processes), illustrating commonalities in approach. Often most interesting to students is the idea that modes in diagonal relationship on the model seem to attend to and value opposite things, which can often limit communication, problem solving, creativity, and teamwork when people preferring these modes are grouped together.

After studying this model, students receive personalized assessments of their own "attraction to or aversion for" each of four distinct mental modes. I share my own HBDI™ assessment and the class's averages, encouraging students to share their assessments (which are confidential) with each other as they wish. I stress that individual results are "neither good or bad or right or wrong" (Herrmann, 1995, p. 76), but indicators of personal preferences. The training also emphasizes that preference for a mental mode is not the same as competence in it (not liking math is no excuse for not doing well in it!). These personal profiles are used repeatedly throughout the term to discuss strategies for better learning, course selection, choice of major, career possibilities, and other advising functions.

When we begin work on the semester-long web page project, I emphasize the importance of the four mental modes in communication, teamwork, and relationship development. The model teaches that each individual has a unique combination of preferences but that individuals with similar profiles often share tendencies. People are drawn to others who "speak their language," who discuss subjects of shared interest and who value the same types of "proof." In this early part of the term, we practice identifying the use of the mental modes through close analysis of articles and speeches, identifying preferences in each, noting how certain communication strategies resonate with some members of the class and not with others. We also analyze popular entertainment, discuss television shows, movies, and even amusement park rides in terms of mental modes to which each activity appeals. Students practice operating in each mental mode, including those they least prefer, to heighten their understanding of what other thinkers value. They do this both through in-class paired exercises ("selling a stereo" to a partner who is assumed to prefer the mode that the seller least prefers) and in writing (arguing something they believe using only evidence from the mode they least prefer). Feedback comes from peers and from me.

Also during this preparation phase, students receive training in the second skill: critical thinking about fact, proof, and bias. This ties in well with the ideas introduced via use of the HBDI™. I work in conjunction with a college librarian to provide students with a targeted introduction to the college resources, both paper and electronic, that investigate multiple sides of contemporary cultural questions. These include sources such as the *Opposing Viewpoints* series of texts and the *CQ Researcher* online periodical. Following that, we study one contemporary critical issue together, analyzing arguments using the Whole Brain Model™, learning to identify fact and bias, and studying what sorts of information each thinking style considers as valid proof. The rubric used is a "Communication Walk-Around" (Herrmann, 1996, p. 119) that guides students with specific questions to evaluate the communication elements valued by each thinking style. I observe to see whether they can identify different thinking style biases and, as we progress, whether they can imagine different ways to convey the same information to appeal to a broad audience, including people who prefer to think in all four ways. This practice is assessed in class through peer and instructor feedback and through short written assignments.

The third skill introduced to students is increased computing competence using a particular web page design software, Dreamweaver. In fewer than three total hours (distributed over several class periods) I provide students with minimal training in the basics of setting up a simple web page with links and graphics. As a model, we study the college's daily news web page (one with which they are all familiar) that is built with the same tools they have learned. With their new knowledge, they analyze this page and learn how they too can build a professional-looking web presence. Each student practices making a simple set of pages in class, with working links, graphics, and some manipulation of fonts and colors.

These first five weeks of the term focus on assessment of the sort that Herman, Aschbacher, and Winters (1992) describe as the first monitoring purpose of assessment (as summarized by the North Central Regional Educational Laboratory, 1994): "to determine whether or not students have acquired specific knowledge or skills. The assessment should focus on the products of student learning using selected answer tests (such as multiple choice) and direct assessment of projects and student products." By the end of this portion of the semester, students have demonstrated their abilities to themselves and to me in the three skill areas. As the class moves on toward the larger project, I can adjust small instructional units or even individualized ones as needed to help students further develop the skills they need to succeed (understanding multiple ways of thinking; thinking critically about fact, proof, and bias; and increasing computing competence). As a result, students move toward the larger project with an enhanced sense of self-confidence about what they can do.

The Web Page Project

During the skill development and modeling work of the first few weeks, students also investigate and narrow topics for the larger project. This work requires an investigation of sources available through the college library and online, including a review of several web sites. For this students use the "Evaluation Criteria" provided online by the New Mexico State University Library (Beck, 1997). In addition, students narrow their topics according to these instructions: "Choose a contemporary controversial issue about which at least three possible points of view exist." Then they must narrow that issue into one focused "yes, no, or maybe" question. To shape this question, students must first move beyond a phrase that names a topic without any sense of value judgment and form a question that implies value judgment. In other words, a student cannot select "eating disorders" as a topic or even "causes for eating disorders in teenage girls." However a student might use "Do beauty pageants cause eating disorders in contestants or in those who admire contestants?" or "Do high school teachers and coaches provide preferential treatment to thinner women, thus indirectly adding to the pressure that can cause eating disorders?"

After students have constructed a question, confirmed available sources, and secured my approval, they begin the web page assignment. This is highly structured in its content. Because the students tackling the assignment are all first-term students, and because approximately half of them are not concurrently enrolled in a freshman academic writing course, I do not assume that they have familiarity with constructing research projects in any meaningful way. Providing them with an outline for content allows students to focus on communicating their findings in ways that take into account all four of the mental models introduced in the HBDI™, on creating appropriate content, and on designing appealing and user-friendly web sites.

To achieve all of this, I break the larger web page assignment into six distinct components, listed here with the instructions I give to my students for each (note that each has specific references to the thinking styles we've studied):

1. The timeline: This is A quadrant information (just the facts with dates and headlines or short sentences) presented in a B quadrant format (an orderly timeline). You want to research the history of your issue (often you'll need to look back into history for some context), including the most important events so that your web site user can get a sense of your topic with a fairly quick look. If you want examples of how to do this, visit the library reference section and look at one of the many historical timeline books. These will give you good ideas

for content and method of presentation (how can you make such B quadrant stuff interesting to a D quadrant visual thinker?).

2. The links: You may find many, many links to groups, individuals, movies, scientists, etc., with fascinating information on your issue. You must sift through them and select the two that you think are the best for each side of your issue. You will provide the title of the web site and the address, a short explanation of whom the site represents and what is included there. Then, please include a short paragraph based on the web evaluation materials explaining to your users why you've included each site. Please note: This means at least four web sites total in the links section. Think about A quadrant information sifted into a D quadrant overview for your paragraphs. And consider the C quadrant sense of relationship as you illustrate links (literally and figuratively) between these sites.

3. The pro and con essays: As part of your web site, you will need to write two short essays: one summarizing the arguments on the pro side of your issue and one summarizing the arguments on the con side of your issue. The most important thing to remember as you write these pieces is that you must keep yourself absent from the text. These sections are not about your opinion (that's later, I promise). In these sections you want to present yourself as a solid, trustworthy, fair, even-handed researcher. You need to write each piece doing your best to make that side look smart and sensible and correct. When your web site users read these parts of your site, they should not be able to see your personal opinion. This is fundamentally A quadrant stuff (facts and more facts); though you may present information or quotes from all quadrants, your attitude must be that of the detached scientist.

4. The my side essay: At last! Here is the section of your web site where you can present your opinion on the issue. Be sure that you draw from and link to the infor-

mation you have presented in the time line, links, and pro and con essays. You may do this in any format you like as long as you achieve the goals of this portion of the web site: Express yourself. Be respectful. Be passionate. Depict yourself as educated and thoughtful. Urge others to action. You'll want to include "proof" as defined by thinkers in all four quadrants so that your opinion has the broadest appeal to readers.

5. The my action essay: This section of your site tells about the action you took (why you selected it, what you did, what resulted, what you learned). It should urge others to take action as well (even if the action is different than your own). Previous students have written letters to editors, sponsored children in other countries, taken polls, passed out flyers, called congress members, spoken bravely in dorm meetings, and so on. Present it however you want as long as you meet these goals for the broadest possible audience.

6. The overview: This is the last part of your web page you'll write, but the first thing your visitors will read. Think of this as the entry page to your web site. It should quickly let users know about the content and structure. It should have links to the various parts of your project (my side, my action, pro, con, and so forth). It should be appealing and inviting and set the tone for the rest of the site—for all users. So as you revise it, consider all four thinking styles.

The work-assessment-feedback-work loop in this class is actually more like an ascending spiral than a loop. I create staggered due dates for each component, and each component's instructional time includes a content and writing workshop with peer editing groups and a design workshop in a computer lab with peer groups and technical support. Therefore, each student receives two rounds of informal assessment and feedback on each component before I formally assess it for a grade. At that time, I provide written feedback on printouts of their web pages with comments

designed to help students revise each component before publication to the web and to do better work on the next component. This also allows for the second purpose for assessment
as described by Herman et al. (1992) and summarized by
the North Central Regional Educational Laboratory (1994):
"to diagnose student strengths and weaknesses and plan
appropriate instruction."

When I perceive weaknesses in a significant number
of students, I design a mini-lesson that can boost those
skills, which I then include in the next class period. A mini-
lesson is "a short, focused segment of a larger curriculum
unit" (Harris & Hodges, 1995, p. 154) that explicitly provides skill and strategy instruction followed by immediate
application. It usually lasts only about 10 to 15 minutes.
Students dig right into the mini-lessons because they are
immediately relevant to and useful in the next component
they must complete. In addition, discussion and questions
during these mini-lessons can be among the best of the
course: Students have studied closely the work of other
students and received comments from their peers, and so
they have a breadth of ideas to think about as they consider
the content and design of their next project component. By
the time they reach their third and fourth components, students are, for the most part, turning in polished work.

There is an eighth component to the project: a review
of the final polished web projects as wholes. Approximately
two weeks before the end of the term, the projects, with all
revisions, are due. Students turn these in on CD-ROM, and
I upload them to the course web site where they are available
to the college community. (The finished web sites are published to the college community only, a restricted publication
necessitated by the copyright rules for many of the image
resources students use in their projects. Instructors doing
a project like this would be well served by reviewing image
use copyright with their librarians because the rights of use
purchased by each library can vary.) After this publication,
I assess each project for a holistic grade, worth roughly the
same number of points as any one component but empha-

sizing the need to polish each piece of the project even after it is individually assessed. Students who fail to revise and attend to overall design and coordination score low here. Before I added this component, many students failed to follow through with a final polish; now they do much better. In addition, it allows me a comprehensive look at the students' accumulated abilities in all the skills of the course: understanding multiple ways of thinking; thinking critically about fact, proof, and bias; and increasing computing competence.

One final aspect of the project remains: public presentation with formal peer evaluation. I provide a chart assigning each student three other students' projects for review. I also provide a rubric for that review, which asks the reviewer to focus on the author's ability to address all four thinking styles in content and design, to provide fact without bias in appropriate sections and valued "proof" for all thinking styles, and for overall appeal and ease of use through technical design. These are, of course, the three skills we built throughout the course. Students write these peer reviews and bring them to class during the final class periods. In those classes, students present their own projects to the class and the reviewers lead discussion—not on the contentious issues at stake, but on the three skills. Discussion follows the components of Roger Firestien's (1996) rubric, the PPC: first we discuss the *plusses* of a project, then the *potentials*, then *concerns*, with suggestions for improvement. Most conversation focuses on the use of communication skills as explained through the HBDI™ training. How well does each web project demonstrate the author's knowledge of and ability to appeal to the four distinct methods of communication? How well are those balanced? Does this web site include materials that would appeal to thinkers of all preferences? Features that might attract or put off certain kinds of thinkers are noted.

Conclusion

The advantages of creating a cumulative semester-long project like this are obvious, particularly in terms of assessment.

By the time students finish this course, their work on the project has received a minimum of 15 separate assessments from me and other students. The skills learned in the first part of the course are transferred and synthesized into a new context during the creation of their web projects. This is an assessment tool that has built into its design continued student engagement: content, shape of assignment, multiple significant decisions, public product, built-in audience of peers—all of these encourage skill development and provide a complex way for them to demonstrate their mastery.

In addition, this structure allows me to frequently gather information about my students' learning so that I can adjust my instruction as needed. Within a term, I can create mini-lessons to meet specific needs, guide discussions to highlight unclear material, revise assignment instructions, and make other modifications to help students perform to the best of their abilities. This in turn improves student learning and engagement because they know exactly what the goals are, how they are doing, and how they can improve.

Finally, I find that this focus on one assignment built across several stages provides me with a more satisfying pedagogical experience. Rarely do I feel as if I have to move on to something new while some students have failed to grasp an essential skill of the course. I enjoy the structure that allows students to revise work for reassessment right up to the end of the course when the web pages are published. I learn by listening in on the frequent peer assessment, not only about what my students have grasped of course content, but about their *Aha!* moments: how the thinking theories have begun to change their perceptions of friends and classes and even what they watch on television; how they reframe their experiences in other classes in the context of new ideas about proof; how their environments challenge their ability to learn and learn well. Thanks to their creative and unique connections, I learn more about them and their world; knowing that, I revise the course for them and, with their help and insight, for future students as well.

References

Angelo, T. A. (1991). Ten easy pieces: Assessing higher learning in four dimensions. In T. A. Angelo (Ed.), *New directions for teaching and learning: No. 46. Classroom research: Early lessons from success* (pp. 17–31). San Francisco, CA: Jossey-Bass.

Beck, S. (1997). *The good, the bad & the ugly: Or, why it's a good idea to evaluate web sources.* Retrieved May 7, 2007, from the New Mexico State University Library web site: http://lib.nmsu.edu/instruction/evalcrit.html

Firestien, R. L. (1996). *Leading on the creative edge: Gaining competitive advantage through the power of creative problem solving.* Colorado Springs, CO: Pinon Press.

Harris, T. L., & Hodges, R. E. (Eds.). (1995). *The literacy dictionary: The vocabulary of reading and writing.* Newark, DE: International Reading Association.

Herman, J. L., Aschbacher, P. R., & Winters, L. (1992). *A practical guide to alternative assessment.* Alexandria, VA: Association for Supervision and Curriculum Development.

Herrmann, N. (1995). *The creative brain.* Lake Lure, NC: Ned Herrmann Group.

Herrmann, N. (1996). *The whole brain business book.* New York, NY: McGraw-Hill.

North Central Regional Educational Laboratory. (1994). *Match assessments to the purposes for assessment.* Retrieved June 13, 2007, from www.ncrel.org/sdrs/areas/issues/methods/assment/as7purp.htm

Walvoord, B. E., & McCarthy, L. P. (1990). *Thinking and writing in college: A naturalistic study of students in four disciplines.* Urbana, IL: National Council of Teachers of English.

9

Demonstrating Synthesis: Technology Assessment Tools for Field Experience Learning

Susan Cherup

At my institution, field experiences are fundamental to connecting college course content in the teacher education program to real world P–12 classrooms; each education course has an integrated field experience. These field experiences assist pre-service teachers in learning the day-to-day practice of teaching by simultaneously preparing them for the realities of the teaching profession and by connecting theory to practice. For example, one pre-service teacher exclaimed that her field placement mentor had invited her to attend an Individualized Educational Planning team meeting, something she had recently learned about and discussed in the college classroom. This experience helped her make the connection between real-world experiences and college coursework. Such experiences give validity to coursework and bridge the huge chasm between theory and practice. This chapter will explain the process of using technology as a tool for the assessment of field placement learning by faculty and students and will lay out the benefits to pre-service teachers and professors.

History of the Traditional Journal Assignment

For as long as I can remember, a student's self assessment, field experience mentors' evaluations, and the professor's evaluations were combined to outline specific ways in which pre-service teachers were to improve their field performance, to increase their pedagogical content knowledge base, and to fine-tune their personal skills in the journey toward becoming *highly qualified* (under the No Child Left Behind Act) and successful teachers. Part of the student evaluation included lengthy journals submitted at various times throughout the semester. A range of information was included in these journals: time spent in the placement, the nature of the pre-service teacher's involvement and activities, the content of the P–12 class, explanations of the theory-to-practice continuum, a review of professional articles relating specifically to the setting, technology applications observed in the setting, and the pre-service teacher's self-evaluation of performance. In the end, the candidate was also expected to clarify goals for the next field placement (Weimer, 2002). The time-consuming task of reading and evaluating these journals was left to the professor. When the journals were returned, some students read the comments written by the professor and took them seriously. Others simply looked at the grade and tossed the journals in their backpacks. In some cases, this *feedback* was merely a physical exchange of a notebook between student and professor. What became of the journal was a mystery. Did it serve to improve student performance? Was it ever looked at again? Ironically, the *professor* may have benefited the most from this assignment as he or she learned about approximately 50 articles from professional literature that had been reviewed by a class full of students. In addition, these journals, though tedious to grade, served as a checkpoint to determine if pre-service teachers were meeting the Entry-Level Standards for Michigan Teachers (ELSMT) in the area of written expression.

NETS*T Guide Change in Traditional Journal Assignment

When the National Education Technology Standards for Teachers (NETS*T) were issued, describing what teachers should know and be able to do with technology, my colleagues and I realized that we needed to merge a technology component with the more traditional assessments verifying student understanding and skills in these placements. Doing so would also broaden and deepen the students' level of preparation for the teaching profession.

> Assessing only a classroom teacher's knowledge and ability to use basic technology skills misses the key feature of technology in teaching and learning—that when effectively used, technology empowers students to improve conceptual understanding and learn content in deeper and richer ways than ever before. (International Society for Technology in Education, 2003, p. 1)

The field placement assignment changed from a written journal to a classroom multimedia presentation. Using the same information requirements, students create an electronic version of the field placement journal. Rather than a single journal entry submitted only to the professor, students now deliver a multimedia presentation to professor, peers, and invited guests. In effect, the student takes on the role of teacher. Written and oral expression is combined with a technology component resulting in a professional public articulation of field experience knowledge and skills: knowing and doing. This multilayered presentation has become the new vehicle for the assessment of field experience learning. As a result, assessment has become more reflective, interactive, and comprehensive. Assessment now includes how effectively the student presents the information and the design of the multimedia format, as well as the original content requirements. Students' performance is assessed to determine if it has reached the required levels of proficiency in both the ELSMT and the NETS*T. Additionally, feedback from peers, the professor, and the pre-service teachers themselves allow for a more authentic assessment of professional knowledge. After all, this is what teams of teachers do in classrooms to solve problems every day.

While assessment of the field experience learning has expanded and the demonstration of students' knowledge and experiential learning changed, the basic procedures have remained the same. Students continue to select field placements in the usual way. During the second week of the semester, pre-service teachers in my Exceptional Child course select placements from a range of available settings that accommodate their schedules and availability of transportation. For example, students can choose to work in a special education day school or in a general education classroom that includes students with disabilities. Another might select a resource room, or one could decide to work one-on-one in an after school program with a student with autism. After two weeks in the placement, each student publicly shares basic details of the field placement: location, student population, mentor, initial reactions, and so on. This verbal, active process serves to alert all members of the course to the range of placements and the diversity among the children and adults in the settings. We continue to use a written midterm and final evaluation by the field placement mentor in addition to the new electronic self-evaluation by the pre-service teacher.

Changes that Make a Difference

The multimedia presentations that are developed during the semester are given to peers, the professor, and invited guests at the end of the semester. These presentations include the same requirements that were written in the journal: time spent in the placement, level of the pre-service teacher's involvement, the content of the P–12 class, explanations of the theory-to-practice continuum, a review of professional articles relating to the setting, technology applications observed in the setting, students' self-evaluation of performance, and goals for the next field placement. A significant difference is that assessment now includes presentation skills: visual contact with the audience, suitable use of gestures, appropriate posture, clear communication, professional terminology, effective speaking, and the presenter's level of confidence (see Table 9.1). The assessment also includes the students' proficiency in meeting the NETS*T I, III, IV, V, and VI (for updates and information see http://cnets.iste.org/teachers).

In the presentation, pre-service teachers become "real" teachers. They teach their peers about their placements; they navigate web sites that bring their research alive; they link class content to actual P–12 settings; they explain and show, through web sites, specific technology applications useful to large and small student groups as well as individuals (i.e., assistive technology); they show video clips; and they respond to questions from peers and the professor. As a result, this assignment transforms the presenter from a scribe writing for a limited audience—the professor—into a professional teacher.

Technology has provided a holistic way for students to demonstrate what they have learned and can do in their field placements. These multimedia presentations allow peers to compare their field experiences to those of the presenter, thus broadening the learning for every member of the class. Instead of the professor being the only one to benefit from the students' field experiences, everyone hears and learns about the placements.

Chalk & Wire for Storage, Assessment, and Portfolios

Through the web-based program Chalk & Wire, adopted by the education department at my college, technology now provides a place for students to store these multimedia presentations and for professors to enter data on the performance of pre-service teachers. The journal notebook may have been tossed in the backpack or possibly the wastebasket, but the multimedia presentation has instead found a home in what we call the "storage bin" of Chalk & Wire. Students upload their multimedia presentations and evaluations from mentor teachers, professor, and peers into Chalk

Table 9.1 Assessment of Presentation Skills

	Excellent 4 points	Proficient 3 points	Developing Proficiency 2 points	Unsatisfactory 1 point
Eye Contact	Establishes eye contact with everyone in the room.	Establishes eye contact with most people in the room.	Establishes minimal eye contact.	Does not look at people during the presentation.
Gestures/Posture	Stands up straight and uses natural and effective gestures.	Generally stands up straight and uses gestures.	Either stands up straight or gestures are somewhat limited, unnatural and/or stiff.	Slouches and uses unnatural gestures or no gestures.
Communication	Communicates knowledge and experiences in an exceptionally clear, organized, detailed, and integrated manner using professional terminology.	Communicates knowledge and experiences in a clear, organized, detailed, and integrated manner using professional terminology.	Communicates knowledge and experiences in a somewhat clear, organized, detailed, and integrated manner using limited professional terminology.	Limited communication of knowledge and experiences and lacking professional terminology.
Speaking	Speaks in an exceptionally clear and articulate manner without using slang, "umms," "okays," etc.	Speaks in a clear and articulate manner with minimal use of slang, "umms," "okays," etc.	Speaks in a somewhat clear and articulate manner with minimal use of slang, "umms," "okays," etc.	Limited clear and articulate speech.
Confidence	Looks relaxed and confident.	Appears somewhat relaxed and confident.	Appears nervous and somewhat confident.	Nervous and lacks confidence.

& Wire. For example, the final evaluation from the mentor teacher is uploaded into the Chalk & Wire program by the pre-service teacher, and the professor enters the level of recommendation from the P–12 mentor evaluation into the department database. Mentor rating choices include *highly recommended, recommended, recommended with reservations,* and *not recommended.* This process makes it relatively easy for the department to ascertain the number of students performing at any given level. Similarly, the professor enters the evaluation of the multimedia presentation into Chalk & Wire, and another determination is made of the student's level of competency. All education faculty use ratings based on the rubric descriptions: *excellent, proficient, developing proficiency,* and *unsatisfactory.*

The process of saving these artifacts begins in one of the first courses in the educational sequence, the Exceptional Child class, where students learn to save their multimedia presentation in Chalk & Wire. As students pass through the educational sequence of classes and field experiences, they are continuously saving artifacts that reflect their pedagogical content knowledge and experiences in their Chalk & Wire storage bins. Finally, using the stored information, students are able to readily construct their student teaching portfolios.

Assessment of the multimedia presentations allows the department to gather data on professional dispositions, pedagogical content knowledge, and progress in meeting the ELSMT and NETS*T. Over time, we are able to make judgments about the efficacy of the program, to make adjustments as needed, and to advise individual students about areas in need of attention. These assessments can be easily viewed at any time from any computer to determine pre-service teachers' progress over time.

Using Assessment for Program Accountability

A growing task for teacher education programs includes systematically gathering, storing, and analyzing data on student performance in both academic and field placement settings. At the college level these data are used to provide evidence that each pre-service teacher is meeting the national and state standards required for entry into the teaching profession. External, program, and student assessments are fundamental to teacher education programs. The rigorous requirements of the National Council on the Accreditation of Teacher Education demand a careful look at the assessment of candidates' knowledge and skills in data required by the so-called SPAs—Specialty Program Associations—and all appropriate state standards related to academic majors and minors. Chalk & Wire provides this means for gathering, assessing, and storing student work for later analysis. It is being used to store assessments on student performance, pedagogical content knowledge, and skills over time. Careful examination of these data will guide programs in verifying student performance and adjusting programs to prepare teachers for the 21st century.

Benefits and Challenges to Students and Professors

While assessment of field experiences through journals has been time consuming, multimedia presentations often require more time. Presentations also take away from class time because two class periods per 15-week semester are used. In addition, because it is impossible for every member of the class to present during these two class periods, many presentations have to be scheduled outside of class. For a class of 25 students and a presentation length of 20 minutes, another six to eight hours of outside class time are needed. These hours must be arranged according to students' schedules, the professor's schedule, availability of rooms, and computer access.

However, the benefits of the multimedia presentation far outweigh the challenges. Professional literature is now presented to the entire class rather than read only by the professor in the traditional written journals. Another benefit to both professor and student is the reduction of plagiarism cases: Students need to orally explain the professional articles and their relevance to the field experiences. Students cannot simply copy and paste information into journals. Pre-service teachers either clearly explain the professional literature and its application to the field experiences or they are sorely embarrassed by their poor performance in presenting the information.

In addition, the multimedia presentations allow students to become active listeners, participants, and assessors. Students provide oral and written feedback to the presenters, which adds an additional layer of comments and assessment of professional behavior. Sample comments from a recent semester include the following:

- "All the technology you showed that is vital to your student managing his daily experiences was phenomenal."
- "If you use a dark background, use a lighter/white text on all the slides."
- "Slow down when speaking."
- "Sometimes you moved in nervous ways such as playing with your hair."
- "Nice breakdown between personal and professional goals."
- "Your enthusiasm for being in the classroom is obvious. Your energy will be an asset."

Because of the active role of the audience, peers pressure pre-service teachers to perform to the best of their abilities in oral and written expression as well as in creative and clear design of the multimedia format. In turn, peers have the opportunity to experience varied presentations that may enhance their own creative skills by seeing others use PowerPoint, personal web sites, and HyperStudio in new and innovative ways. Additionally, peers become active listeners, responsible for evaluating the performance of their classmates and engaging in a question-and-answer period. Peers' evaluations are not a part of the final grade, but they serve to give honest and useful feedback to the presenters. Using this approach to peer evaluation leads to frank and open remarks, improved performance, and actual experience in the daily work of teachers.

Multimedia presentations have the potential to encourage self-improvement. The components and nature of this self-improvement become part of the daily diet of class discussion. Periodic review of personal performance, the data that back up that performance, and the range of input from individuals help students understand improvement or the lack of improvement over time. Frequently this level of input motivates students to increase their own level of engagement in the field placement setting. This is more effective than the professor telling them to do so and stating the benefits.

The multimedia presentation offers the pre-service teacher the opportunity to become the teacher, to model theory in pedagogical practice well before taking up one's own P–12 classroom. Through this experience the student comes to better understand the role of the teacher and whether the profession is an appropriate career choice. Instructors do not need to wait for the student teaching experience to learn or discover this important detail. Teaching peers, the professor, and invited guests, as well as fielding questions, provide another checkpoint in the process of becoming, or not becoming, a teacher.

Perhaps the most important outcome of the multimedia presentation is the intrinsic value it has for the pre-service teacher. Well-researched, rehearsed, and reflective pre-service teachers complete the presentation knowing they are headed for the right profession.

References

International Society for Technology in Education. (2003). *Resources for Assessment.* Eugene, OR: Author.

Weimer, M. (2002). *Learner-centered teaching: Five key changes to practice.* San Francisco, CA: Jossey-Bass.

10

Assessing an Engineering Design Team Project: Build It, and They Will Come

Michael Misovich, Roger Veldman

Most engineering curricula include one or more capstone design courses in which students complete a major design project. In these courses, students are expected to use their understanding of mathematics, science, and engineering analysis to produce some practical and tangible result. This result may be a physical device or prototype, as is often the case in mechanical engineering of a machine component or electrical engineering of a microelectronic device. For large-scale design projects where a prototype is not practical, the result may be a description of the design in sufficient detail for construction or further analysis, such as civil engineering of a highway project or chemical engineering of a petroleum refinery.

Such a capstone design course is intended to reflect a typical industrial environment or similar situation in engineering practice, where complex, open-ended problems are solved by project teams. Objectives of such a course may include functioning as a member of a design team, using basic project management techniques, experiencing an open-ended design problem, establishing detailed design requirements, designing a device or system to meet these requirements, properly documenting project results, and practicing communication skills. Many of these objectives are difficult to assess using traditional instruments such as exams and short homework assignments, or even essays. Assessment in a capstone engineering design course makes direct use of the natural work outputs and documentation of the design process. These may include presentations to various audiences, written materials such as reports and design notebooks, and construction of a physical prototype. Approaches for teaching capstone design, typical course objectives, and assessment methods have been summarized by some recent studies and surveys (e.g., Campbell & Colbeck, 1998; Dutson, Todd, Magleby, & Sorensen, 1997; McKenzie, Trevisan, Davis, & Beyerlein, 2004; Todd, Magleby, Sorensen, Swan, & Anthony, 1995).

Course assessment in engineering programs is further constrained by program accreditation considerations. One criterion used for accreditation of engineering programs in the United States by ABET, the Accreditation Board for Engineering and Technology, includes a list of program outcomes. These outcomes, shown in Figure 10.1, "are statements that describe what students are expected to know and be able to do by the time of graduation" (ABET, 2007, p. 1). The criterion also requires "evidence that the results of this assessment process are applied to the further development of the program" (p. 2).

It is possible to make use of a capstone design course to assess all of the outcomes in Figure 10.1, as some engineering educators do (Chase, 2006). This has the advantage of assessing the outcomes just prior to graduation when the course is usually taken, which gives a valid measurement of students' abilities by the time of graduation. Indeed, some of the outcomes in Figure 10.1 may only be expected of students in a capstone design course and nowhere else in the curriculum. One disadvantage of this approach is the time delay in course improvement for those outcomes that are developed early in the curriculum. In other cases, those outcomes that are specific to the design course are the focus of course assessment there. Conceivably, only outcome (c) could be evaluated. In practice, outcomes (d), (g), (h), and (k) also may be a focus of assessment in the design course. Felder and Brent (2003) have compiled an extensive list of references for assessing each of the outcomes. Finally, the

Figure 10.1 ABET Engineering Program Outcomes

(a) An ability to apply knowledge of mathematics, science, and engineering
(b) An ability to design and conduct experiments, as well as to analyze and interpret data
(c) An ability to design a system, component, or process to meet desired needs
(d) An ability to function on multidisciplinary teams
(e) An ability to identify, formulate, and solve engineering problems
(f) An understanding of professional ethical responsibility
(g) An ability to communicate effectively
(h) The broad education necessary to understand the impact of engineering solutions in a global and societal context
(i) A recognition of the need for, and an ability to engage in, life-long learning
(j) A knowledge of contemporary issues
(k) An ability to use the techniques, skills, and modern engineering tools necessary for engineering practice

list of outcomes in Figure 10.1 is used by ABET for program assessment purposes but is not required for individual courses. Individual courses retain substantial flexibility in describing outcomes that contribute to the overall program outcomes so long as the linkage between course and program outcomes is indicated.

The capstone design course described here is the second in a two-semester sequence taken during the senior year. In the first course, each student works on an individual design project, limited in scope, which is usually related to his or her own interests. Some examples have included small-scale laboratory devices, improvements or new concepts for household products, or devices used in hobbies such as music or sports. One of the objectives of this first design course is to learn how to plan and carry out an engineering design project from the initial problem definition through completion of a working prototype. Another objective is to develop an ability to use engineering design methods and an understanding of the structure of the engineering design process. Although each student works on an individual design project, the exposure to the steps of the design process and use of design methods is similar for all students in the course.

The capstone (second) design course also includes a project as its principal activity. It differs in nature from the project in the first course in several important ways. Students work as a design team of two to four members. The project is wider in scope and typically more open-ended than the one in the first course. Although each student has a limited amount of choice in project selection, the assignment of students to project teams is done by the faculty member who is teaching the course. The project arises from a request or need from an external sponsor, frequently a local business or industry. During their work on the project, students interact directly with a contact person who is a representative of the sponsor.

The syllabus of the capstone course lists the following course objectives: to learn to function as a member of an engineering design team, to experience an open-ended engineering design problem, to design a device or system to meet given design requirements, to utilize proper engineering documentation of project findings and results, and to practice oral and written communication skills. Course objectives are linked to outcomes (c), (d), (g), (h), and (k) in Figure 10.1 for purposes of program assessment. In this chapter, the terms *design quality, team effectiveness, communication skills, nontechnical issues,* and *engineering tools* will be used to label the outcomes (c), (d), (g), (h), and (k) in that order.

An important feature of the capstone course is frequent assessment and feedback on the design project. Nearly every week each team is required to give an approximately 10-minute project update to the other students in the class and the instructor. Each team gives a 30-minute midterm presentation to the sponsor. The presentations are intended to elicit feedback, which will help each team to make improvements if necessary or to assure the team members that they are making progress. Many of the steps of the engineering design process are cumulative in nature. By incorporating frequent assessment and feedback, students are continuously steered through the steps of the process. This makes it unlikely that a project will turn out to be a complete failure.

In the remainder of this chapter, a case study of one project from the capstone course will be used to illustrate design project objectives and assessment. The purpose of the project was to design a mechanical device to straighten and roll elastic cloth bandages. The sponsor was the college athletic training department, and a group of three engineering seniors was assigned to the project. Their contact person was a faculty member in the athletic training department.

Each of the following sections describes assessment of one of the five outcomes from this design project.

Design Quality

In assessing design quality, meaning "an ability to design a system, component, or process to meet desired needs," it is important to take a broad view of the design process. Assessment should not focus only on the quality of the product or prototype but should encompass all the steps of the process culminating in the prototype. The prototype bandage roller device, shown in operation in Figure 10.2, did indeed function well.

Figure 10.2 Student Operating Bandage Roller Device

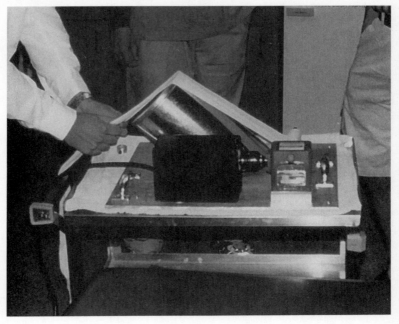

Design quality may be assessed by breaking down the complex process of engineering design into individual steps. The first step is problem definition, which involves interaction between the design team members and the sponsor. The goal of this step is to draft a set of comprehensive design requirements for the project. Table 10.1 shows the design requirements developed for the bandage roller by the student team. Each requirement is given both as a qualitative word or phrase and as a quantitative measurement if possible. The team also weighted the requirements to indicate their importance.

When requirements are identified, they become an important part of the assessment of design quality in two ways. First, as an initial step in the design process itself,

Table 10.1 Design Requirements for Bandage Roller

Qualitative	Quantitative	Weighting
Economical	Costs less than $200	15
Rolls flat	Zero wrinkles or folds	15
Does not damage bandages	Zero marks or tears	10
Easy to operate/ control	One person operation	10
Quick	One bandage per minute	10
Rolls tightly	No more than 5% larger than hand rolled	10
Aesthetically pleasing	All machinery encased	10
Portable	Weight less than 10 pounds	5
Durable	Capable of 5,000 rolls	5
Variable speed	50 to 350 rpm	3
Compatible	Works with 2- to 6-inch width and length up to 10 yards	

the requirements may be evaluated for completeness, clarity, practicality, and relevance. Second, the requirements provide a road map for evaluation of the actual prototype when it is constructed. The team should be able to indicate or provide evidence that each requirement was met.

Of the requirements listed for the bandage roller, probably the most difficult to evaluate in the student design course is the durability requirement that the device be capable of 5,000 rolls. (It would be quite suitable, and indeed necessary, as a requirement in industrial design practice where some type of automated testing equipment might be available for the purpose.) Another problem with this requirement is its lack of clarity. Was the intention that the device operate for 5,000 rolls before routine maintenance such as lubrication, or before replacement of worn parts, or would the entire device need replacement after 5,000 rolls?

With one or two exceptions like this one, the bandage roller requirements shown in Table 10.1 illustrate a good set of requirements.

Following the statement of design requirements, concept generation is the next step in engineering design. Common practice is to break down the operation of a device into functions and to apply creativity or brainstorming techniques to discover alternative ways of performing the functions. Some type of evaluation process must then be applied to choose among the alternatives, resulting in a conceptual design. After a conceptual design has been chosen, the design and its components are tested, refined, and improved until a detailed design is prepared. It is important to fix the basic design concept fairly early in the process and work on refining the details. A common error among engineering design students is not settling on a concept early enough to leave time for detailed design. A related error is making major concept changes late in the design process.

In the bandage roller design, the project team settled on a conceptual design quickly. It consisted of four major components: a motor, a speed reducer, a spooler, and a flattening device. The team was aided by the insight of the sponsor, who had used similar devices in the past and was aware of some of their limitations. In particular, including a flattening device was expected to speed up the rolling process. The team identified a bottleneck in device operation because the bandages were both wrinkled and twisted from laundering. Some simple experimentation indicated that it would be easier to implement a method to flatten a wrinkled bandage than to untwist a bandage.

When the conceptual design including these components was fixed, the team put its effort into developing alternatives for each component. The most interesting design process occurred for the flattening device. A rough prototype with a motor and spooler was assembled for purposes of testing various concepts for the flattening device. Team members brainstormed to select a variety of objects and shapes for this testing phase. Some of these included fingers, brushes, and dowels. Interestingly, their tests demonstrated that the shape that worked best was that of an automobile side rear view mirror housing that had been left in the design workroom by another student group. Further experimentation revealed that this shape worked so well because of three main characteristics: a sharp leading edge, a convex gently curved surface, and a smooth trailing edge. After searching for other objects with these characteristics, the group located a metal grain scoop at a local farm supply store that cost less than two dollars. The scoop was adapted to become the flattener for the bandage roller prototype.

The remaining components of the device required less design creativity than the flattener but still posed a variety of challenges for the team. Initially they had intended to directly turn the spooler with the motor, but the combination of a relatively low speed for operator control and relatively high torque for stretching the bandage was not possible with a conventional off-the-shelf motor. The team decided to purchase a standard universal AC motor that operated at 5,000 rpm and focused their effort on designing a speed reducer. Later during troubleshooting of the prototype device, they determined that the purchased motor was overheating and another motor from an electric drill was substituted and found to be suitable.

Both the spooler and the speed reducer components also required some design experimentation and choices among alternatives. The design team attempted to use an inexpensive gearing set for speed reduction but found it lacked durability. Eventually an industrially rated gearbox was used; however, this component cost more than $200.

In assessing the design process steps from concept generation through detailed design and prototype construction, the instructor focused on whether the team had accomplished the appropriate steps in the proper order. Among the strengths of this project were the conceptual design of the flattening component and the extensive testing of other components.

The team also followed the design procedure by selecting a concept and sticking with it during detailed design.

Perhaps the biggest weakness of the design, as the team members admitted in their final design report, was the speed reducer component. Although it was extremely durable, this component alone caused the design to fail to meet its cost requirement. The root cause of the problem was in the step where the design team evaluated speed reducers. They had initially considered both gear-driven and belt-driven speed reducers, and the rough prototype used in early testing of flattening components was a belt-driven system. Although the team included cost as one of the highest weighted requirements for the overall device design, they failed to consider it in their analysis of the speed reducer component. This was one of the few aspects in which the team's conceptual and detailed design process was not effective. Nearly all of the remaining requirements in Table 10.1 were easily achieved or in the end were determined not to be crucial to the quality of the design.

A final step in the design process was the assembly and final testing of the device and delivery to the sponsor. As previously mentioned, the prototype bandage roller device did satisfactorily perform the desired function. It was delivered to the sponsor at the college athletic training office where it has been used intermittently for several years with no problems. The instructor's assessment of design quality for this project on a 1 to 4 scale (poor, fair, good, excellent) was 3.7, or just below excellent. It ranked in the top quarter of design projects in the capstone course in a recent four-year period. The principal basis for this assessment was the quality of the design process and methods used, not merely the acceptable functioning of the device.

Team Effectiveness

Assessment of team effectiveness in the capstone engineering design class is based on a variety of factors. It is likely similar to assessment of team effectiveness in other classroom settings. Two important characteristics of effective design teams are shared responsibility for the progress of the team as a whole and participation by all team members. Another characteristic of effective design teams is having members who assume different roles and responsibilities based on their individual skills and abilities. In the design course, the instructor relies on observations of the team in group settings, especially presentations, to draw conclusions about team effectiveness. Written feedback about the contributions of all team members is solicited from each student individually near the conclusion of the project.

The instructor's assessment of team effectiveness for the bandage roller project team was 3.0, or good. This team was cohesive and had a good sense of shared responsibility. Their weakest characteristic was assuming different roles and responsibilities. This is common among students in design teams, and one way to improve learning of this aspect of team effectiveness is to explicitly remind student teams of it throughout the project. For example, in addition to giving feedback on technical aspects of design during the weekly project updates, it is possible to point out positive or negative examples of effective teaming.

Communication Skills

As was the case with team effectiveness, assessment of communication skills in the capstone engineering design class is similar to other classroom settings. In the design course, there are several opportunities for students to demonstrate both oral and written communication skills. Project teams produce a written formal design report for the sponsor and the instructor. A final presentation is given to the sponsor and is also given at a department seminar attended by faculty and undergraduate students. A midterm presentation is given to the sponsor. Finally, weekly progress reports are given to the instructor and to class members working on other projects. Although it is not required, the students in project teams typically divide up all presentations so that each member explains the portion of the project with which he or she is most familiar.

Evaluation criteria for the written design report include mechanical correctness of writing, appropriate tone and style for a formal report, report organization, and completeness of both the body of the report and supporting material provided in appendixes. The report should be complete in its breadth by describing all the steps of the design process. It should also be complete in its depth by thoroughly documenting the details of each step so that the work could be reproduced, checked, or modified by a practicing engineer with general knowledge of the subject. Often the documentation will include detailed mathematical calculations, extensive tables or lists, graphs, charts, and scale drawings, which are placed in appendixes. It is common for the appendixes of an engineering design report to be longer than the body of the report.

Oral communication is assessed using similar criteria of mechanics, tone and style, and organization. Some additional evaluations are made on the quality of visuals, effective speaking, the ability to answer questions, and audience awareness. For example, although the final presentations given to the sponsor and to the undergraduate seminar will be similar, each should be tailored to emphasize items that are important to the specific audience.

The bandage roller team received an assessment of 3.4, between good and excellent, for their communication skills. This ranked in the lowest third of project teams in the capstone course for a recent four-year period, yet it was quite acceptable. The average assessment score of all teams for communication skills during this period was 3.6, substantially higher than the scores received for the other four assessed outcomes. A likely explanation for this result is the repeated opportunities for students to practice this outcome in the course and receive feedback. Many of the engineering students also participate in summer research or industrial internships where they receive experience in oral and written communication of technical material prior to their senior year. Finally, students in the capstone design course have had many opportunities to learn and practice communication skills in earlier courses in engineering and in the general education curriculum.

Nontechnical Issues

This refers to "the broad education necessary to understand the impact of engineering solutions in a global and societal context," and it is probably the most difficult of the five broad outcomes to assess with the capstone design project. The major work products of the project—the prototype, the design report, and the presentations—emphasize a goal-seeking process rather than the reflective thinking needed to understand the nontechnical impact of the project.

Still, there are certain details that may be incorporated into the design process or at least documented in the report. These may include a discussion of the environmental impact of mass production of the prototype, a lifecycle analysis of issues involving waste products and recycling, human factors considerations such as ergonomics or convenience of use, or considerations related to health and safety of manufacturing employees or of consumers of the product. Relevant issues may differ depending on the type of engineering design being done. For a mechanical device, ergonomics and safe manufacturing practices are frequently important considerations along with solid waste disposal and recycling. In the design of a chemical processing facility, concerns may focus on the environmental or health impact of raw materials or byproducts.

The bandage roller team received an assessment of 3.3, somewhat above good, for the consideration of nontechnical issues in their project. This ranked among the top quarter of design projects in recent years. An especially strong characteristic of the bandage roller project was the attention paid to human factors. The device was designed not merely to work well from a technical standpoint but also to be easy and safe to use and aesthetically pleasing. Intentional decisions to accomplish these ends were made during the design process and documented well in the report. For example, one of the design specifications was that moving parts be encased, contributing both to visual aesthetics and to safety. Other choices were made when designing the motor and speed reducer specifically to improve control for the person operating the device. Among the weaker details of this project was the lack of consideration of any broader impacts such as solid waste disposal or use of components that could be recycled. The team did discuss one additional positive impact of the bandage roller in their report. After introducing a mechanical device into what had been a tedious, labor-intensive process, student athletic training interns were able to spend more time attending to patients and practicing techniques.

A disadvantage of assigning a different capstone project to each student team is the possible inconsistency in the opportunity to consider nontechnical issues in the design. Individual projects naturally integrate these issues to varying degrees. Other projects in recent years with similar high assessments for this outcome were a series of two projects that were designed as a portable feeding mechanism for a large chemical reaction vessel in a pharmaceutical plant. These projects also were strong in considering human factors in the operation of the device and had a significant safety component.

Engineering Tools

Students in the capstone design course have the opportunity to demonstrate their ability to use a variety of "the techniques, skills, and modern engineering tools necessary for engineering practice." This may include traditional techniques and skills such as use of machine shop tools, or it may include modern engineering tools such as computer aided design (CAD) software and computer simulation tools. Evidence for use of these techniques, skills, and tools usually is placed in the appendixes of the design report.

Use of the machine shop may be documented by a detailed description of the fabrication of a component. This should be at a level of detail that would serve as instructions for a person skilled in machine shop usage to reproduce the part. Frequently, CAD software is used to produce scale drawings of three-dimensional components, and these drawings should be included as well. Other computer simulation tools may be used in design work in specialized fields of engineering. Some examples would be mechanical analysis of the stress distribution on an object, electrical analysis of current and voltage in a complex electronic circuit, chemical process analysis of reactions and separations in a refinery or chemical plant, or plant layout analysis in an industrial or civil engineering application.

The bandage roller team received an assessment of 3.0, good, for their use of engineering tools. Their report included a detailed appendix describing the fabrication of the spooler component in their design. Both a CAD drawing and a photograph of the component were present. The main factor preventing the assessment from being higher was the lack of additional documentation of the use of additional computer software or other modern engineering tools. For example, a problem with component layout related to alignment of the motor and gearbox was described in the body of the report. It would have been appropriate to use CAD software to analyze and correct this, or at least to describe the final design layout with a drawing, but the group did not do so. Another concern was the lack of engineering analysis in selecting a motor and speed reducer combination, which resulted in the substitution of three different motors and two speed reducer gearboxes before the prototype was completed. It should be noted that the prototype was successful; however, proper engineering analysis of these components might have avoided considerable troubleshooting and expense in prototype production.

Like the assessment of nontechnical issues, the assessment of use of engineering tools is dependent on the nature of the project itself. Certain projects require more computer analysis or extensive machining and fabrication whereas others present more challenges in concept generation, troubleshooting, or other aspects of design. In recent years, some project topics that have received high assessments on this measure have included design of a robotic vehicle, measurements of drag coefficients with a wind tunnel, computer-aided measurements of vibration, and temperature measurements. Yet during the same period of time, other projects with significant potential for use of engineering tools received the same assessment score as given to the bandage roller. These included a second robotic vehicle design and a computer-interfaced radio frequency identification "smart card" application.

A final interesting observation is that these two outcomes—engineering tools and nontechnical issues—were the only pair of the five outcomes to show a correlation. It was a negative correlation, meaning that projects that were more successful at demonstrating the use of engineering tools were less successful at demonstrating consideration of nontechnical issues, and vice versa. Some of the characteristics of the projects that rated highly for use of engineering tools were discussed in the previous paragraph. An additional characteristic was that the prototypes designed in these projects were typically intended for research purposes, not for mass production or for use by an operator or consumer. Often the student team members themselves were the only operators or users of the devices.

Conclusion

A team engineering design project in a capstone course provides an opportunity for assessment of several outcomes that are considered to be important in the course and in the overall program. The assessment is made on the natural work output of the design process, namely, a prototype of a product or a description of a process. Although the functioning of the device is an important consideration, many of the evaluation criteria are related to communication and documentation of the design process by a formal written report and by oral presentations.

Frequent project updates allow for timely feedback to the students, promoting continuous improvement in the quality of the design—the prototype product—and in the quality of communication and documentation. When the final report and presentations are prepared at the end of the semester, the quality is typically high. Because much of the material was prepared in a cumulative fashion during the semester, the task of producing these final items seems less onerous to the students.

An advantage of using projects from external sponsors is that assessment may be done in a context that is representative of an industrial environment or engineering practice. A possible disadvantage is that the needs of an external sponsor on a particular project may not align completely with all of the outcomes to be assessed. This may introduce some inconsistency when assigning a different project to each student team. By requiring each team to frequently present updates to the whole class, this becomes less of a concern. The entire class is exposed to all of the situations faced by individual teams.

Similar approaches to assessment are possible in many disciplines where a project-based capstone course is used to integrate student learning from various courses. Some institutions require capstone experiences in many or all majors (Shapiro, 2002). Interesting parallels to design of an engineering prototype are seen in contexts of artistic expression where fine art objects or performances are the natural work product. Some capstone courses in the natural or social sciences include major research projects. Although the goal is not analogous to producing a prototype device, the creative process of designing and implementing a research project has many parallels to the process of engineering design. A major similarity exists in the process of communication and documentation of the project results.

Project-based courses in any discipline allow several learning outcomes to be assessed in a natural way that exemplifies practice of the discipline. The cumulative nature of a major capstone project provides opportunities for frequent feedback and continuous improvement. The placement of a capstone project near the completion of the curriculum allows students to demonstrate their abilities, integrate their learning from various courses, and build their confidence as they enter a career or graduate school. Senior design projects provide a strong direct assessment of outcomes related to design quality, team effectiveness, communication skills, and nontechnical issues.

References

Accreditation Board for Engineering and Technology. (2007). *Criteria for accrediting engineering programs.* Retrieved May 9, 2007, from www.abet.org/Linked%20Documents-UPDATE/ Criteria%20and%20PP/E001%2007-08%20EAC% 20Criteria%2011-15-06-PROPOSED.pdf

Campbell, S., & Colbeck, C. L. (1998, June/July). *Teaching and assessing engineering design: A review of the research.* Paper presented at the 106th annual American Society for Engineering Education Conference and Exposition, Seattle, WA.

Chase, R. (2006, February). *Effectively linking the evaluation of senior capstone projects to the assessment process: A direct measurement method.* Paper presented at Best Assessment Processes VIII, Terre Haute, IN.

Dutson, A. J., Todd, R. H., Magleby, S. P., & Sorensen, C. D. (1997). A review of literature on teaching engineering design through project-oriented capstone courses. *Journal of Engineering Education, 86*(1), 17–28.

Felder, R. M., & Brent, R. (2003, January). Designing and teaching courses to satisfy the ABET engineering criteria. *Journal of Engineering Education, 92*(1), 7–25.

McKenzie, L. J., Trevisan, M. S., Davis, D. C., & Beyerlein, S. W. (2004, June). *Capstone design courses and assessment: A national study*. Paper presented at the 111th annual American Society for Engineering Education Conference and Exposition, Salt Lake City, UT.

Shapiro, D. (2002). Improving teaching and learning through outcome-based capstone experiences. In A. Doherty, T. Riordan, & J. Roth (Eds.), *Student learning: A central focus for institutions of higher education* (pp. 49–52). Milwaukee, WI: Alverno College Institute.

Todd, R. H., Magleby, S. P., Sorensen, C. D., Swan, B. R., & Anthony, D. K. (1995). A survey of capstone engineering courses in North America. *Journal of Engineering Education, 84*(2), 165–174.

11

Tracking Learning Over Time in Health Care Education Using Clinical Proficiency Transcripts

Richard Ray

The next time you are ill or injured and need the services of a health care professional, ask yourself what that practitioner's employer really knew about that person's mastery of basic skills prior to his or her being hired. As the nurse prepares to insert an intravenous line into one of your body's blood vessels, ask yourself if the hospital knew if she could perform this skill at a basic, intermediate, or advanced level before she was assigned to work on your case. Did the athletic trainer who is helping you rehabilitate from knee surgery master the necessary skills while he was in college to avoid damaging the surgical repair? When the radiographer who is about to expose you to a dose of ionizing radiation graduated from college, to what degree did she master the skills required to provide you with the minimum amount necessary for your procedure?

Chances are, you can't answer any of these questions. Unfortunately, the agencies that employ these health care professionals can't either. At best, they may be able to tell you that the nurse earned a B+ in her Nursing Practicum course, that the athletic trainer earned an A– in his Therapeutic Exercise course, and that the radiographer earned a C+ in her Imaging Techniques course. Employers are at the mercy of the colleges and universities that educate their employees to assure that the skills they need to be able to provide high-quality patient care have been mastered by the time they graduate. Regrettably, health care education programs in these colleges and universities are

often ill prepared to state with confidence what their graduates know, can do, and value—and to what degree. This
chapter describes a system—the clinical proficiency transcript—that helps students, educators, and employers better understand the degree to which health care program
graduates have mastered the critical elements required for
safe and effective professional practice.

Learning Over Time and Assessment

Central to the concept of mastery (of knowledge or skills)
is the idea that students learn over time (Amato, Konin,
& Brader, 2002). This learning begins with basic concepts
and skills and should progress over time through increasingly more complex levels. This is important for both basic
and applied sciences (Seymour, 2004). A variety of instructional techniques—each appropriately matched for the level
of learning desired—should be employed in the learning
over time model. For example, physical therapy students
might learn gross anatomy at the recall or recognition
level through a series of lectures in the first year of the
program. By the time they begin their clinical experiences,
however, they will have to be able to synthesize information about a particular patient's anatomic variations with
the signs and symptoms exhibited by that patient—all in
the context of that patient's particular life circumstances.
The instructional methods required to develop mastery at
this level of learning are much different than the lectures
used to develop recall. Case studies, simulated patients,
and directed observations would likely be used at this stage
of the learning over time continuum.

Complex learning requires a variety of intermediate
steps. Accomplishing these steps in a planned, sequenced
fashion in ways that both the student and multiple professors will know exactly where the student is in the process
at any point in time can be a significant challenge. Keeping
track of dozens of students in multiple cohorts requires a

commitment to thinking differently about student assessment. Grades on a transcript become less meaningful when one considers this level of pedagogical complexity.

Clinical Proficiency Transcripts

A clinical proficiency transcript is a tool that serves several purposes, including 1) documentation of completion of health care education program requirements, 2) documentation of the number and type of clinical experiences, 3) documentation of mastery of clinical proficiency modules, and 4) indexing the contents of the student's portfolio (see Figures 11.1, 11.2, 11.3, and 11.4).

Documentation of Program Requirements

Every health care education program has a complex mix of didactic and clinical requirements, some that are reflected in required courses and others that are not. Many of these

Figure 11.1   Courses Taken and Grades Earned Portion of the Clinical Proficiency Transcript

Name of Student		**ATHLETIC TRAINING PROGRAM AUDIT**	
Courses Taken and Grades Earned			
Intro Psych	Fall 02 B+	Exercise Phys	Spring 03 A–
Statistics	Fall 01 B	Exercise Phys Lab	Spring 2004 A
Cells & Genetics	Fall 02 C+	Prevention & Care	Fall 03 B+
Human Phys	Fall 02 B–	Practicum 3a	Fall 03 A
Human Anatomy	Spring 03 C+	Practicum 3b	Spring 2004 A
Practicum 1a	Fall 02 A	Therapeutic Modalities	Fall 05 A–
Practium 1b	Spring 03 A	Therapeutic Exercise	Fall 05 A
Health Ed	Spring 05 A–	Assessment	Spring 2004 B–/B–
Safety, 1st Aid, CPR	Fall 02 A	Ath. Train. Admin.	Fall 03 A–
Anatomical Kines	Fall 03 A	Medical Aspects of Sports	Spring 05 A
Practicum 2a	May 2003 A	Practicum 4a	Fall 05 A
Practicum 2b	May 2003 A	Practicum 4b	Spring 05 A
Nutrition	Spring 03 A	Health Psych	Fall 03 B

Figure 11.2 Clinical Experience Section of an Athletic Training Program Clinical Proficiency Transcript

		Clinical Experiences	
High School Internship	Fall 2004	Case Studies	Sports Experiences
Sports Med Clinic Internship	Spring 2004	Fall 02 3rd metatarsal fx	Men's Track
Medical Office Internship	Winter 04–05	Spring 03 Bimalleoloral ankle fx	Women's Track
Other Internships	Summer 04 Denver Broncos	Spring 05 Plantar warts	Women's Soccer
Surgery Observation 1	Dec 03 ACL Reconstruction	Spring 05 Shoulder pain	Men's Basketball
Surgery Observation 2	April 04 Knee debridement, menis …		Baseball
Administrative Experience 1	Spr 04 NCAA ISS BA		Football
Administrative Experience 2			Men's Soccer

Clinical Hours Sorted by Experience Type

FB Total Hours	41	VB Total Hours		High School Total Hours	89
MSOC Total Hours	193	WGOLF Total Hours		Sports Med Clinical Total Hours	46
MXC Total Hours	3	WSOC Total Hours	289	Medical Practice Total Hours	28
MGOLF Total Hours		WXC Total Hours	6	General Ath. Train. Hours	295
MLACS Total Hours		WSWIM Total Hours	12		
MSWIM Total Hours	12	WBB Total Hours	3		
MBB Total Hours	227.5	WLACS Total Hours	3		
MTEN Total Hours		SB Total Hours			
MTRK Total Hours	77	WTEN Total Hours			
BA Total Hours	84.5	WTRK Total Hours	77		
GYMNAST Total Hours		ICEHKY Total Hours			
WRSTL Total Hours					
TOTAL CLINICAL HOURS AS OF					

Figure 11.3 Competency Module Mastery Section of the Clinical Proficiency Transcript

Competency Modules	Date Completed	Competency Modules	Date Completed
Module A 1 Admin. Pol. And Proc.	9/19/2002	Module H 1 Rehab. Overview	5/5/2005
Module A 2 Injury Record Keeping	9/15/2002	Module H 2 Rehab. Adherence Motivation	5/52005
Module A 3 Ath Trm Supplies	9/15/2002	Module H 3 Range of Motion Flexibility Exer.	5/16/2003
Module A 4 Ath Trm Cln Equip–Sm	9/15/2002	Module H 4 Joint Mobilization	5/29/2003
Module A 5 Ath Trm Cln Equip–Mjr	1/24/2003	Module H 5 Isometric Resis. Exer.	5/21/2003
Module B 1 Implement Emer Action Plan	9/19/2002	Module H 6 Isotonic Strength Trn Devices	5/21/2003
Module B 2 Cardio. Resus.	1/21/2003	Module H 7 Daily Adjust. Progress. Exer.	5/23/2003
Module B 3 Choking, Hemorrhaging, Shock	1/21/2003	Module H 8 Isokinetic Dynamometers	5/27/2003
Module B 4 Emer Transp.	4/22/2003	Module H 9 Muscular Endurance	5/23/2003
Module B 5 Med. Svcs	3/4/2003	Module H 10 Aquatic Therapy	5/28/2003
Module B 6 Rest, Ice, Compression, etc.	9/26/2002	Module H 11 Neuromusc. Control/Coordination	5/27/2003
Module B 7 Open Wounds	9/26/2002	Module H 12 Muscular Speed Exer	5/23/2003
Module B 8 Univ. Precautions	9/26/2002	Module H 13 Agility Exer.	5/23/2003
Module B 9 Enviro. Injury/Illness	9/26/2002	Module H 14 Plyometrics	5/27/2003
Module B 10 Anaphylaxis/Asthma Attacks	5/9/2003	Module H 15 Cardio. Endurance	5/23/2003
Module B 11 Poison Control Center	1/24/2003	Module H 16 Activity-Specific Skills	5/23/2003
Module C 1 Ankle Taping	9/27/2002	Module J 1 Foot Injury Mngmnt Module	9/23/2003
Module C 2 Knee Taping	5/7/2003	Module J 2 Ankle Injury Mngmnt	10/14/2003
Module C 3 Thigh/Lower Leg Taping	10/29/2002	Module J 3 Lower Leg Injury Mngmnt	10/29/2003
Module C 4 Foot Care Taping	4/3/2003	Module J 4 Knee Injury Mngmnt	11/19/2003
Module C 5 Hip/Abdom Taping	10/17/2002	Module J 5 Thigh Injury Mngmnt	4/29/2004
Module C 6 Shoulder Taping	5/7/2003	Module J 6 Hip Pelvic Injury Mngmnt	4/29/2004
Module C 7 Elbow to Wrist Taping	4/1/2003	Module J 7 Thoracic Lumbar Spine Injury	4/7/2004
Module C 8 Hand/Finger Taping	4/10/2003	Module J 8 Thorax/Abdominal Injury Mngmnt	4/1/2004
Module C 9 Head/Neck Taping	5/7/2003	Module J 9 Shoulder Injury	9/29/2004
Module D 1 Anthropo. Measure/Screen	5/9/2003	Module J 10 Arm/Elbow/Injury Mngmnt	11/5/2004
Module D 2 Protective Equip Fitting	5/7/2003	Module J 11 Wrist/Hand Injury Mngmnt	12/1/2004
Module D 3 Developing Flexibility	5/16/2003	Module J 12 Cervical Spine Injury Mngmnt	4/27/2005
Module D 4 Strength Training	5/21/2003	Module J 13 Head/Facial Injury Mngmnt	4/27/2005

Figure 11.4 Generic Clinical Proficiency Rubric

Bony and Soft Tissue Palpation Skills

Name_____   Practicum Level_____   Module Number_____

Skill Assessed_____   Clinical Instructor_____

Instructions for clinical instructors: Use this check sheet as part of your assessment for the skill listed above. This sheet should be used to assess only the psychomotor aspect of the competency module. Cognitive and affective aspects of the module should be assessed using other methods, including written exams, case studies, and projects. Keep this check sheet until the student has successfully mastered the entire competency module. When the module is complete, sign and date the student's master competency file and his or her copy of *Knight*. This check sheet can be given to the student for his or her records at that time.

The skill components included on this check sheet are considered to be the minimum required for successful completion of a bony and soft tissue palpation task. Since this is a generic check sheet to be used for all bony and soft tissue palpation tasks, you may wish to add other skill components that you think are important for a specific task.

	Pass	Fail	Pass	Fail	Pass	Fail
			Skill Component	Date: First Attempt	Date: Second Attempt	Date: Third Attempt
Patient positioned properly						
Patient dressed and draped appropriately						
Structures assessed for point tenderness						
Structures assessed for edema						
Structures assessed for tissue continuity						
Structures assessed for crepitus						
Structures assessed for temperature						

continued on next page

Figure 11.4 Generic Clinical Proficiency Rubric (*cont.*)

	Pass	Fail	Pass	Fail	Pass	Fail
Appropriate structures identified						
Bilateral assessment performed						
Assessment findings properly recorded as a SOAP note						
Additional Skill Components						
Skill 1						
Skill 2						
Skill 3						
Skill 4						
Specific Structures To Be Palpated						
Structure 1						
Structure 2						
Structure 3						
Comments:						

programmatic elements are sequenced in such a way that certain clinical experiences are linked so that information learned in a didactic course can be applied in a clinical setting. This connection is sometimes contemporaneous but may also be separated by a semester or more. The clinical proficiency transcript provides students, faculty, and clinical instructors with knowledge of what the student has accomplished and what requirements remain to be completed. The closer the student gets to the end of the program, the more important this purpose of the clinical proficiency transcript becomes.

Documentation of Clinical Experiences

The standard academic transcript available from the registrar's office at any college or university does a good job of documenting the courses students take and the grades earned in those courses. The clinical proficiency transcript serves this purpose as well, but it goes one step further. It also documents the number, type, nature, and timing of the experiences where health care students apply their learning (see Figure 11.2). This is helpful for several reasons. First, it provides university-certified proof of a student's clinical experiences—an increasingly valuable commodity in this age of increasing resume fabrication. Second, it helps clinical education coordinators plan future student assignments. This can be a challenging task in large programs that use a widespread network of off-campus clinical education placements.

Documentation of Clinical Proficiency Modules

One of the most powerful elements of this transcript is the component that documents students' mastery of the various clinical proficiencies required for safe and effective health care practice. The National Athletic Trainers' Association (2006) states that "the intent of a Clinical Proficiency is to capture the essence of learning over time by documenting a student's progression from cognitive competence and psychomotor skill performance through supervised clinical application as evidenced by the integration of decision making and critical thinking." Clinical proficiencies are sometimes contained completely within a single course. However, because most clinical proficiencies include a progression of learning over time, many span several courses. Competency mastery may take place in a traditional course or in a clinical field placement. Mastery may be assessed by a regular faculty member or by a clinical instructor hundreds of miles away from the campus (see Figure 11.3).

The standardized rubric used to evaluate competency mastery (see Figure 11.4) should document the elements of the proficiency examination, the number of attempts, and the dates of those attempts. When successfully completed, the information is recorded on the clinical proficiency transcript. The rubric shown in Figure 11.4 is one of 12 generic instruments used to evaluate skill mastery in an athletic training education program. This sample is designed for evaluation of bony and soft tissue palpation skills. It can be modified for any body part and is therefore useful across a variety of courses in the typical athletic training curriculum. Furthermore, individual instructors can modify it to reflect special points of emphasis contained in their courses. This model allows for hundreds of skills to be evaluated with just a handful of appropriately modified generic rubrics. Data regarding the number of attempts— either for entire skills or subsets of skills—can be analyzed across cohorts. When used this way, these instruments become powerful assessment tools that can form the basis of meaningful curricular reforms.

Indexing the Student Portfolio

The clinical proficiency transcript can also serve as a useful index of learning products in the student's portfolio. The transcript is constructed using a computer database. The various fields can be modified to reflect the range of student exams, papers, projects, presentations, and other learning products commonly used in health care education programs. As each item is placed in the portfolio, it is first entered into the database and onto the clinical proficiency transcript. A quick glance at the transcript will help inform faculty and students which elements have been completed and which are yet to be accomplished.

Software Solutions

Clinical proficiency transcripts can be built with paper and pencil. However, using a computer database allows easier access to the information by multiple users. Databases also simplify the creation of reports used for a variety of purposes. The simplest computer application for building the clinical proficiency transcript is probably a spreadsheet program like Microsoft Excel. For greater data manipulation and reporting ability, a database program that allows the user to define fields is a better choice. Microsoft Access and FileMaker Pro are two such examples. A third option is to use a business contact management program like ACT! This software comes with predefined fields for commonly used information like name, address, phone number, email address, and so on. It also allows for user-defined fields that can be used to enter data specific to program completion requirements, competency module completion, and clinical experience data. The predefined reports are customizable and are what will be used to build the actual clinical proficiency transcript. Another option available to colleges and universities that use Banner or similar information management systems is to enter the data used to build the clinical proficiency transcript into these powerful centralized repositories of campus data. The advantage to this approach is that the student's contact information and course grades will already be in the system and won't have to be rekeyed into a secondary database. The disadvantage to this approach is that it requires more up-front support from the campus computing staff because the interfaces are often not very user-friendly. Another drawback is that multiple layers of permission are normally required to create fields, build reports, and access various kinds of data.

How to Use the Clinical Proficiency Transcript

There are at least four ways that clinical proficiency audits can be used to improve student learning in health care education and in certain other forms of higher education: 1) student audits, 2) academic advising, 3) improved communication with clinical instructors, and 4) program assessment.

Student Audits

One of the uses of the clinical proficiency transcript is as a periodic audit of student progress toward graduation. Transcripts can be printed or emailed to students at the conclusion of each semester so they can see what they have accomplished and what requirements remain to be completed prior to graduation. For programs with large numbers of clinical requirements, this can be very useful in preventing misunderstandings and miscommunication because the student can see what is left to be done at the end of each semester.

Academic Advising

The information contained on the clinical proficiency transcript is also useful for helping students plan their programs. When faculty and students can look together at the same time and see what elements of both the didactic and clinical parts of the program need to be accomplished, the advising process becomes much easier. The transcript is also a very useful device when advisors are asked to write letters of recommendation for graduate school or for employment because they can see at a glance the entire range of a student's clinical experience.

Improved Communication with Clinical Instructors

As mentioned earlier, health care education programs often use large networks of hospitals, clinics, and other health care agencies to deliver at least a portion of the clinical experience component of their programs. Each clinical site can have multiple instructors, each of whose primary role is to provide patient care. The less time these clinical instructors have to spend getting up to speed regarding each student's background and competence, the better. The clinical proficiency transcript is a helpful way to communicate what students know and can do when they arrive for the first day of their clinical experiences. This tool often saves time and reduces the risk of miscommunication between the clinical education coordinator, clinical instructor, and student.

Program Assessment

A creatively constructed clinical proficiency transcript can be a powerful source of program assessment. If the data from students' clinical experiences are properly categorized and entered, they can be retrieved at any time and analyzed to help answer questions about how well students are learning. For example, depending on what kinds of information are included in the database from which the clinical proficiency transcript is produced, the following questions could be answered:

- Which clinical proficiencies take our students the longest time to learn?
- Which clinical proficiencies are the most difficult to learn?
- Which clinical experiences require the most time from our students? Which require the least time?
- What is the correlation between successful and timely accomplishment of certain clinical proficiencies and the grades earned in corresponding courses?

The database used to create the clinical proficiency transcript must be designed with these questions in mind if it is to serve as an effective assessment tool. Furthermore, the greater the flexibility to move data around in the database and to create new fields, the more useful the clinical proficiency transcript will be in the assessment of student learning.

Conclusion

Clinical proficiency transcripts can serve a variety of useful functions in health care education. In addition to providing a much richer source of information on student abilities than the standard course transcript, they also help break down barriers to communication between faculty, students, and widely dispersed clinical instructors. They can be powerful aids in the assessment of student learning. When used in conjunction with other tools and methods, they can help students, their teachers, and their employers understand with greater confidence what entry-level health care professionals know, can do, and value when they leave the academy and enter the clinic.

References

Amato, H. K., Konin, J. K., & Brader, H. (2002). A model for learning over time: The big picture. *Journal of Athletic Training, 37*(4 suppl), S236–S240.

National Athletic Trainers' Association. (2006). *4th ed. competency FAQs: Clinical proficiencies.* Retrieved May 9, 2007, from http://nataec.org/Committees/ProfessionalEduca tionCompetencies/4thEdCompetencyFAQs/tabid/94/ Default.aspx

Seymour, E. (2004). *Emergent strategy for the assessment of student learning over time.* Retrieved May 9, 2007, from www.pkal .org/documents/StrategyForAssessmentOfStudentLearn ing.cfm

12

Verbing the Noun: Grammar in Action

Rhoda Janzen

Many English instructors will agree that in recent years there has been no small amount of controversy about how to teach grammar at the college level or indeed if it should be taught at all. I argue that it should be taught and that it can be taught better than we have been teaching it. After summarizing some of the key issues that have made the teaching of grammar such a tendentious subject in recent years, I will describe two kinds of creative assessment that I have developed for a popular grammar course at the small liberal arts college where I teach. I've chosen to describe these two kinds of assessment because they reprise the larger goals of the course: to help students practice standard grammar usage in academic and professional writing; to demonstrate that grammar doesn't have to be boring; to promote creative pedagogy; and to encourage students to recognize and challenge cultural assumptions about grammar.

These days most discussions about grammar begin with a quick disclaimer about what we mean when we say *grammar*. The disclaimers, so the hope goes, function as a preemptive strike against accusations of elitism that buzz like gnats around the subject. Alas, declaring that there are three kinds of grammar does not mitigate the offensiveness of the unspoken assumption in many conversations about grammar pedagogy. I might summarize the assumption like this: Privilege makes the rules. This assumption needs to be made visible in every critical conversation about the teaching of grammar, and I will return to this subject later.

But back to the three basic categories agreed upon by grammarians. First we have Grammar 1, the unconscious knowledge of grammar that all of us share whether or not we can name the parts of speech (Gribbin, 1996). Grammar 1 is learned informally by everyone who can speak or write so that even nonstandard English-speakers have grammatical knowledge. For example, if a speaker says, "She hurtin'," the speaker has followed a syntactical script without which the same speaker might have uttered, "Hurtin' she." Gribbin defines Grammar 2 as "conscious knowledge of language structures including concepts, terminology, and analytical techniques" (p. 55). If I hold forth on the compelling subject of nonrestrictive relative clauses, or if I roll away the stone from the tomb of diagramming, then I've got Grammar 2. But the controversy lies in Grammar 3, which is constituted by all of the markers of linguistic etiquette that govern correct and incorrect usage.

In "Teaching Grammar" Marlene Asselin (2002) summarizes the chief ideological controversy, noting that "the chosen standard is that of the cultural elite, therefore necessitating formal learning by those whose Grammar 1 is not the standard" (p. 52). Asselin identifies the pedagogic challenge like this: "to teach the 'code of power' to all students to assure their opportunities in the world in which that code dominates" (p. 52). I have often heard scholars defend Grammar 3 as a needful lubricity, something that oils the creaky wheels of a civilized world. A grammarian once told me that usage rules are as vital as traffic regulations. We'd have chaos without them! I objected to the comparison, though. If we abandoned Grammar 3 and besprinkled our writing with commas according to whim, would we not still understand one another? Without traffic regulations we might die. But what is the worst that could happen if we did away with comma regulations?

Theoretically, nothing. But the problem is that we deal with reality, not theory. Bad things may indeed happen if we do not assist our students to learn the etiquette of standard English. Eighth-grade English teacher Melissa J. Engel (2001, p. 105) describes an exchange she had with a frustrated student:

Student: What will labeling the parts of speech ever do for me?

Engel: You need to know the parts of speech in case somebody walks up behind you in an alley and asks, "Quick, what's the adjective in the following sentence?"

This exchange, which occurred three weeks into Engel's first teaching job, set her thinking about the relevance of teaching the parts of speech at all—in what sense, exactly, was this a useful activity? By article's end, Engel concludes that we have indeed ". . .been asking our students to complete meaningless labeling exercises for too long" (p. 107). She suggests that a more meaningful way to teach grammar occurs in the context of a student's own writing.

I can think of another answer to the student's question, one less amusing and much scarier. My answer to the reluctant student would have been this: "When you go to apply for a job, your cover letter will be chucked if you can't tell an adverb from an adjective." Gone are those hopeful days when optimists believed that our students would magically absorb correct usage from their reading and from the standard English spoken around them by parents, teachers, and media figures. Magic absorption hasn't happened. Perhaps this rosy scenario might have worked if there hadn't been a powerful seismic shift between written and spoken English; student knowledge of written conventions has dropped abruptly off the continent, like California in the Big One. How can we expect our students to know an adjective from an adverb when every morning chipper newscasters across America say, "Now a real quick look at the weather"?

Anyone who has been teaching over the last 20 years has noticed the disappearance of Grammar 2 and the marked downshift of Grammar 3 in student writing. Freshmen arrive at college congratulating themselves on their high SATs, peacefully unaware that they have not mastered the basic unit of written communication, the sentence. The so-called worst Grammar 3 errors—fragment, comma splice, and run-on, worst because they send the signal of functional illiteracy—appear even in essays written by our brightest and our best. When did this happen? *Why* did it happen?

Kolln (1996) documents the change, tracing it back to 1963, when in the Richard Braddock Report, Braddock, Richard Lloyd-Jones, and Lowell Schoer marshaled evidence not only that the teaching of formal grammar did not improve student writing, but that it actually *harmed* student writing. Kolln reviews the oft-cited research conducted in the 1970s, most of which turned on one simple question: Does studying grammar have any bearing on how well students write? The most frequently cited studies concluded that it did not and that teaching grammar was therefore a waste of time. But the studies themselves were problematic. Vavra (1996) points out that it is "not even necessary to demonstrate the lack of validity" (p. 32) of the research because one of the researchers, Frank O'Hare, subsequently published a writer's handbook that devoted a third of its content to traditional grammar. "If O'Hare doesn't believe in the validity of his own study," asks Vavra reasonably, "why should anybody else?" (p. 32).

After the Braddock Report, when grammar diminished as a curricular priority, the English discipline began to examine product less and process more. As scholars like Peter Elbow and Frank O'Hare moved toward an emphasis on epistemic writing, teachers began to concentrate more on *how* students were conceiving and revising their work. This changing pedagogy collided with the previous pedagogic model in which students' grammatical and rhetorical choices had played a key role in classroom lessons. Martinsen (2000) describes the resulting conflict as a "virtual Woodstock in the English classroom" (p. 123), a free-for-all grammar melee that confused students and permitted teachers to retreat from formal grammar praxis. Now in the 21st century the debate about how best to teach grammar continues. However, there does seem to be a consensus about what *hasn't* worked: striking grammar from the curriculum.

In spring 2002 our college heard some negative feedback about our graduates who were being hired as teachers in area schools. Hiring institutions were expressing concern that our grads couldn't teach grammar. Worse, they didn't *know* grammar. At an English department meeting our chair asked for volunteers to put together a grammar class. Suddenly the room sank into an uneasy silence. I learned later that many of my department colleagues felt that grammar would be difficult to teach because nobody would want to take it. Nobody *would* take it, they said, unless we made it mandatory. And if we made grammar mandatory, students would dread and drag. I disagreed, suspecting that students might actually welcome the chance to learn competence and confidence in their writing.

I've offered Modern English Grammar 13 times since then. It has become one of our most popular courses. Nor is it mandatory: Students seeking teacher certification may take it to fulfill a language arts requirement, but they have other choices that will also meet the requirement. Our English majors may opt for the course as an elective, but they are never required to take it. Interestingly, whenever I have taught the class in the spring and fall semesters, it has been filled to capacity and heavily wait-listed. To meet the demand, my department offers the course both semesters, and I've even started teaching an intensive May term for students who can't fit the course into fall or spring semesters. During and after the course students frequently describe Modern English Grammar not only as their favorite course, but as the most useful course in their entire college experience. Clearly there is a genuine hunger for this material.

Such enthusiasm for grammar is unusual because grammar has historically worn the long white beard of college curricula. What's not to hate? In the old pedagogic models, the ones that faded out long before grammar itself disappeared from public school curricula, grammar was thought to discipline both mind and soul. It functioned as an analog for God's "orderly plan for the world" (Weaver, 1996, p. 15), and instructors presented it as the foundation of all knowledge, the very gateway to secular and sacred understanding (Hillocks & Smith, 1991). Thus, grammar was rendered didactic as well as dull. In these earlier models teachers usually assessed the students' level of grammar acquisition via assignments that called for translation of windy passages from one language to another. Then came the age of rote labeling, of diagramming and sentence combining, all of which invited a punitive professorial response not unlike an old-fashioned slap from the instructor's pointer. This birch-rod response was delivered by the punishing red pen, a venerable metonym for a teacher's scorn. Those of us old enough to have incurred the red frenzy on returned compositions recall how unpleasant that experience can be and how the rules we didn't learn accrued in inverse proportion to the shame we felt. As Murdick (1996) observes,

> Merely red-marking error and covering the text with monotonous corrections and scoldings, as though one mistake were the same as another, represents the kind of careless, indifferent teacher response that causes students to give up, or to protect themselves from criticism by regressing to a simpler, more childish writing style. (p. 43)

How true. In the grammar class that I was developing, therefore, I determined to find a different method than the hectoring red pen. Identifying and labeling student usage errors is a lot like shouting "Boo!" from the margins.

Bonwell and Eison (1991) state that of all the types of peer teaching, it is partnerships and working groups that best "promote the use of active learning in the classroom" (p. 50). In other words, if we want pedagogic innovation in the grammar classroom, we might look to our own student population. Yet this resource was largely ignored in fin de siècle debates regarding the usefulness of teaching Grammar 2—that is, of teaching grammar the old-fashioned way, part by participle. I liked the idea of looking to our own student population to promote the use of active learning; in fact, I thought, I could push that a step further. Why not give the students an active teaching role?

Making student involvement the primary organizing principle in the grammar class seemed the next logical step. My twin goals would be 1) getting students up out of their seats, and 2) tapping into student creativity. What grammar needed was a little motion in the ocean. The first goal would address the yawn factor, and the second would negate the dated stereotype that competence in Grammar 2 could be achieved only through predictable binary pairings: right/wrong, yes/no, teacher/student.

I posited a course component that would help me achieve both these goals, calling it "Grammarama." Teams of students would create an original game that would reinforce some grammar skill set we had learned in the classroom, and then the team would teach the rest of us to play their game. After the game we would debrief as a larger group, discussing what had and had not worked with respect to the group's stated goals for the game. Together we would brainstorm how minor changes in the game might accent different lessons or allow the game to be played with a different age group. Early in the course, when the students first heard about the Grammarama assignment, they would receive a sign-up sheet so that they could group themselves with friends and choose presentation dates compatible with their other academic commitments.

From the beginning, the integration of teaching and playing was central to the syllabus. Students would have plenty of examples that would demonstrate what game playing could achieve in the classroom—and, as already indicated, I wanted students to use their bodies as well as their minds. For example, on the first day of class we begin with the eight basic parts of speech. As soon as students have scribbled down the definition for *adjective,* I hustle them up out of their desks and into a circle on the floor. I tell the students (most of whom plan to become elementary- or secondary-level teachers) that there's a great way to teach children what an adjective is, and that it's easier to show it than explain it. At my instigation everybody begins clapping the thigh-slap, hand-clap, finger-snap rhythm of the children's party game we used to call "Concentration." I've made a few changes to that old game, though, and my students know it by the name "The Senator's Cat." The first step is to model the task. Keeping a slow steady rhythm, I say, "The senator's cat is an *awful* cat." Without missing a beat, the next person has to think of a fresh "a" adjective: "The senator's cat's an *ancient* cat"; "The senator's cat's an *American* cat;" "The senator's cat's an *anal* cat," and so on, until somebody repeats or messes up, at which point we move on to "b" adjectives. We usually play to "f" or so, about 15 minutes. It takes no longer for every player to understand in beautifully concrete terms that if you can say it in front of the word *cat*, it's an adjective. Voilà—lesson learned. Plus there's a bonus: When we hit the "f" adjectives, I can always count on a smarty-pants to offer, "The senator's cat's a *fucking* cat." What a great teaching moment: This contribution usefully shows that even inappropriate curse words subscribe to the same grammatical functions that regulate academic language.

The games always function as a prompt for discussion about pedagogy. For example, immediately after a lesson on what changes a fragment into a sentence, we play a game called "Word Relays." Students group into relay teams who stand in lines in front of the board. In front of each team I write a different five-letter word and shout, "Go!" If a team has the word *train,* the first person runs to the board and writes a word that begins with a "t"; then that person passes the chalk to the second person, who runs to write a word that begins with "r"; the third writes an "a" word, and so on, until a nonsense sentence emerges: Turtles run and interact nicely.

The first team to create a sentence wins, and students have a good time checking and labeling the grammatical components of rival teams' sentences:

[for the word *party*] Poodles anticipate really tiny yoga.
              Subject   verb transitive   direct object

But the greatest value of this activity occurs in the discussion afterward when we see that what makes a sentence is not semantic content but structural syntax. That the sentences are whacky is part of the point. They may often have the cryptic quality of secret passwords (*Pssst! The ship sails at midnight!*), but they are indeed grammatically correct sentences. As a class we discuss how teachers might use this activity in a third-grade classroom and how that lesson might differ from the lesson one would prepare for the eighth-grade classroom.

As the semester advances, the games change to reflect the greater degree of sophistication in the grammar lessons. In the 11th week of a 16-week semester we play a game called "The Glitch-N-Bitch," in which pairs draw five slips of paper from a hat. Each slip bears the name of a specific standard-English usage error—comma splice involving a conjunctive adverb, hypercorrected pronoun, relative clause with no antecedent, and so on—and the pairs must deliberately include one of each of their five errors in a letter of complaint to the business of their choice about the malfunctioning product of their choice. The object is to include these five errors and only these (no unsolicited errors!) and moreover to include them so sneakily that another pair will have difficulty detecting them. When the pairs turn in their creative complaints, students swap letters. Then the students identify and correct the usage errors in the new letter.

Because I have conceived game playing as an integral component of the course, the students are relaxed and eager to participate in the Grammarama assignment. I ask Grammarama groups to turn in a typed description of their games and a description of their goals, praxes, materials, and intended audience. What grammar lesson is the game designed to reinforce? What lessons would precede the game, and what lessons would follow? How could the game interface with other lessons in other subjects? What problems might teachers anticipate, and how might they troubleshoot those problems? How long does it take to prepare the materials for the game? What is the cost of the materials? Are there special considerations of space, noise, supplies, or learning environment?

During the Grammarama presentations, the binary stiffness between professor-teacher is blurred; I enact the role of participating student while the presenters assume the professorial role. Each group member must take an active role in teaching the game to the class and in managing the discussion afterward. Finally, at project's end each group member independently fills out a questionnaire in which that student describes his or her own role in the creation and development of the game. I have found that when students know they will be accountable for this last step, they take their participation very seriously.

I have been amazed and delighted by the Grammarama games my students have created. I have seen games conceived for every level of student, from kindergartners (*Fishing for Verbs* or *Pin the Noun on the Donkey*) to adults (*Dance Diagram Revolution* or *Drink or Diagram*—I hasten to add that my students wisely substituted cream soda for rum in that last one). In the name of grammar I have been asked to turn somersaults, play leapfrog, verb my left noun on a teammate's noun, impersonate a litigator, salute a subordinating conjunction to the tune of *Pop Goes the Weasel,*

and illustrate the meanings of various prepositions by tak-
ing digital photographs of my shoe. Memorable games have
included *Climbing Mount Verbal, Grammar Twister, Feel-
ing a Little Tense, Clausemopolitan, Ghost Sentence, Ouch
Potato, Modal May I, Particle Pursuit, What Not to Swear,
Adverb Charades, Grammar Bites, Verb Turns, The Missing
Link, Grammarpants, In the Beginning Was the Gerund,* and
Vin Diesel Drives Without Cheese.

The second kind of assessment I created for this class
tests the practical application of learned grammar lessons.
I call it "Response Tally." It's a form of evaluation in which
the onus of identifying usage errors shifts from instructor to student, thereby eliminating the punitive red-pen
effect mentioned earlier. Here's how it works. The syllabus
informs students that they can expect weekly response
papers, assignments in which they type one-page responses
to grammar-related prompts. One prompt asks students
to imagine how their families would react if they brought
home a romantic partner who was considerate and kind,
but who in front of the student's family said, referring to the
student, "There ain't hardly nobody nicer alive." Another
asks students to find a friend who has never studied the
basic components of the sentence and then to teach the
friend how to recognize these components: verbs transitive,
intransitive, and linking; direct and indirect objects; and
subject and object complements. I ask students to make
up their own examples rather than borrow the ones from
their class notes. The prompt invites students to describe
this teaching experience. A third prompt asks students to
discuss elitism and privilege as they relate to grammar. Still
another urges students to posit a solution for our collective
curricular problem: Should we just relax our standards for
correct usage given the poor preparation of incoming freshmen and given the strain of already-overloaded freshmen
writing courses? (Naturally I expected that a nonmanda-
tory grammar course would self-select for grammar advo-
cates, but I have been astonished at the pitch of resentment

expressed in these responses. Students are downright angry that they never learned this material in high school, and they overwhelmingly endorse the study of grammar as practical and valuable. Most claim that studying grammar has given them a new confidence in their written and oral communication.)

Response Tally, however, is not about *what* the students write. It's about *how* they write. When I was a graduate student, I took some undergraduate Italian language classes. At that time I was also teaching; I was inspired, therefore, to pay close attention to my professors' pedagogic decisions. I remember thinking that I would have learned so much more from our composition assignments in Italian II if the professor hadn't circled every error I'd made. True, the professor had insisted that we correct our mistakes and resubmit the compositions the next session. But how much more effective it would have been if I had been asked to find my own errors! (I still think that Response Tally would apply superbly as a method of assessment in any foreign language class.)

When my students receive their "graded" response papers from me, all they see is a tally of marks at the top, like this:

$$\cancel{||||} \ ||$$

I explain that each tally mark represents a usage error or a typo, and then I write the grading scale on the board:

    0 errors = 10/10
    1 error = 9/10
    2 or 3 errors = 8/10
    4 or 5 errors = 7/10
    6 or 7 errors = 6/10
    8+ errors = 5/10

Usually that first response paper has a little picket fence of tally marks stretching across the top, and students panic. I tell them, though, that they can rewrite and resubmit these response papers at any time through week 14 but that they have to find the errors themselves. If they can't, I invite them to drop by my office hours and I will help out a bit.

Increasing student accountability has the added benefit of developing the relationship between professor and student. Because of the tally method of assessment, I see virtually every grammar student in my office hours at some point in the semester, and this one-on-one interaction allows me to personalize what I am teaching. It also gives me an accurate sense of where a student needs help most. Some students submit the same response paper four or five times; sometimes they make it worse before it gets better. But there is one thing that they all emphatically learn: There's a big difference between labeling a part of speech and recognizing a usage error in your own writing. In the professional world beyond college, our students will rarely be called on to parse sentences or comment on dependent adverbial clauses. But our students will be expected to deploy sentences free from usage errors and maybe even fix usage errors in somebody else's writing. This is one college assignment that explicitly prepares our students for a future in which they can just say no to bad memos.

There are two caveats about Response Tally, however. The first is that it doesn't work with teaching assistants (TAs). My TAs, no matter how competent their own mechanics, are not up to the challenge of what this style of assessment demands from the instructor. That is, my TAs can usually catch all or most of the usage errors in the students' response papers, but what they frequently cannot do is explain to students what the errors are called or why they are errors. Thus, I arrange for the TAs to practice their grading on quizzes and exams, not on response papers. The second caveat is that the instructor must be absolutely consistent from tally to tally. The instructor needs to decide, for example, that passive voice verbs will *never* be counted as usage errors, or that split infinitives *always* will, or that the relative pronoun *that* simply cannot be used to describe a person.

The final appearance of Response Tally in my course comes at semester's end in the form of a big project, a major component of the course grade. Students present to me a 10-page paper that they have submitted for a grade in another college class. Most frequently this is a paper written in a previous semester. My grammar course is offered as an upper-level elective, so students usually have a nice body of academic research papers from which to choose. In order to avoid an ethically slippery situation, I ask students either to turn in the original paper with the professor's comments and grades written on it, or to have that professor email me confirmation that the paper was indeed submitted for a grade.

For this last assignment, the student revises the entire essay, corrects every usage error and typo, eliminates every redundancy, omits every fatic phrase—in short, tucks in the sheets so tightly you could bounce a quarter on the well-made bed of their prose. Style counts. By semester's end we have covered issues adverting to style (such as active-voice verbs, syntactical variety, and sophisticated punctuation); consequently the assignment becomes more challenging. Well in advance of the due date students receive a checklist of all the tics, goofs, usage errors, and style blunders that frequently compromise the efficacy of academic writing.

Students often register surprise that revising for style and grammar shortens their work. One young woman was tardily chagrinned that she had turned in a 10-page paper that should really have been 2 pages. When students learn how to squeeze the sponge, the professor never has to do this work for them again. I would argue, actually, that the professor should never do this work for them at all. With a nod to the jargon of self-help psychospeak, students need to "own" that which they produce—their work, their grammar, their style or lack thereof. If we fail to teach our students that their grammar usage functions as a cultural semiotic, we contribute to the disenfranchisement of those who have been victimized by dominant power paradigms.

Grammar usage is like body image: People will judge you for it, good or bad, fit or unfit. Because most nonstandard usage errors do not compromise our ability to make ourselves understood, nonstandard usage should, logically speaking, be irrelevant to most professional positions. If an office worker tells you, "Me and my supervisor have both checked the shipment," you will have no trouble understanding the worker's meaning. The worker's usage error does not prevent her from accurately checking the shipment or from lucid communication to her supervisor and to you. In other respects our culture has successfully challenged traditional employment paradigms that once conflated irrelevant categories with professional competence, such as gender, sexual orientation, and race. We have collectively decided that these categories should not have a bearing on an individual's ability to execute his or her job, and we have passed legislation against those forms of discrimination. Thus, the very notion of a standardized grammar, notable for its invisibility in critical conversations about class, race, and gender, is one of the great under-considered inequities of our culture.

In a perfect world we would all be able to speak and write according to our grammar of origin. In a perfect world one sort of grammar would not be touted as better than others. We English teachers may not be able to right a system in which literacy is so closely tied to an elitist standard, but we can empower our students by giving them choices, by giving them information about the grammar they have always taken for granted. The old excuses for not teaching grammar—that it's boring, that it's ineffective—needn't apply. By exercising our own creativity, and by inviting students to tap theirs, we can slay the ghost of grammar past. Grammar does not have to be rote material passively memorized; it can be endlessly inventive and actively played. If we change both our attitude and approach, perhaps our students will understand not only the usage conventions that govern standard English but the power conventions that govern American culture.

Recognizing these conventions involves intellectual work. And that's precisely why it is so important to integrate play. Play is the key to my creative assessment strategy because its lighthearted, spontaneous promotion of student engagement creates a classroom environment in which intellectual work becomes more appealing. I believe that students can learn from play differently than they learn in other ways. Play provides a more nuanced pedagogic method. Play does not replace the traditional work of the classroom (challenging assumptions, thinking critically, learning a body of knowledge); rather, play *extends* this work via a variety of positive experiences. The creation, the incorporation, and the playing of games provide an unusual experience to students who live in a culture that increasingly alienates them from the products of their labor. When else will our students get to see what it is like to test an idea, develop it from start to finish, produce it, perfect it, teach it, *know* it? This pride of ownership achieves many useful outcomes. Play is also a legitimate sort of assessment because it renders academic content more memorable, as my grammar students have often asserted long after they have completed the course. But beyond that, play inspires students to consider intellectual engagement not as a solitary activity but as a social one. It reframes tedious material as exciting; and, because it asks students to be both leader and learner, it instills a confidence that students can transfer to every area of academic inquiry.

Finally, we teachers, too, can transfer play to every area of academic inquiry. It strikes me that the potential application of play as an assessment strategy is wide. With a little creativity, we might see new ways of using play to assess student competence in science, history, and math—in short, in any academic discipline that asks students to memorize terms, rules, dates, and categories. I am reminded of Friedrich Schiller, who at the close of the 18th century argued that some activities endemic to humanity required no validation. Among these was play. In *Letters on the Aesthetic Education of Man*, Schiller (1967) writes, "Man plays only when he is—in the fullest sense of the word—a human being, and he is fully a human being only when he plays" (pp. 106–107).

References

Asselin, M. (2002, June). Teaching grammar. *Teacher Librarian, 29*(5), 52–53.

Bonwell, C. C., & Eison, J. E. (1991). *Active learning: Creating excitement in the classroom* (ASHE-ERIC Higher Education Report No. 1). Washington, DC: The George Washington University, School of Education and Human Development.

Engel, M. J. (2001, March). "What will labeling the parts of speech ever do for me?" *The English Journal, 90*(4), 105–107.

Gribbin, B. (1996, November). The role of generalization in studying grammar and usage. *The English Journal, 85*(7), 55–58.

Hillocks, G., & Smith, M. W. (1991). Grammar and usage. In J. Flood, J. M. Jensen, D. Lapp, & J. R. Squire (Eds.), *Handbook of research on teaching the English language arts* (pp. 591–603). New York, NY: Macmillan.

Kolln, M. (1996, November). Rhetorical grammar: A modification lesson. *The English Journal, 85*(7), 25–31.

Martinsen, A. (2000, September). The Tower of Babel and the teaching of grammar: Writing instruction for a new century. *The English Journal, 90*(1), 122–126.

Murdick, W. (1996, November). What English teachers need to know about grammar. *The English Journal, 85*(7), 38–45.

Schiller, F. (1967). *Letters on the aesthetic education of man* (E. M. Wilkenson & L. A. Willoughby, Trans.). Oxford, UK: Oxford University Press.

Vavra, E. (1996, November). On not teaching grammar. *The English Journal, 85*(7), 32–37.

Weaver, C. (1996, November). Teaching grammar in the context of writing. *The English Journal, 85*(7), 15–24.

13

Hands-On Assessment Can Work for Pre-Service Elementary Teachers

Mary DeYoung

A fundamental rethinking of the teaching and learning of mathematics was set in motion by the 1989 publication of the National Council of Teachers of Mathematics' *Curriculum and Evaluation Standards for School Mathematics*. As teachers began to emphasize conceptual understanding beyond a basic skill level, the mathematical community began to experiment with new ways to measure reasoning and communication skills, thus providing a more complete profile of students' mathematical understanding. Open-ended questions appeared in standardized tests; students of all ages began to justify their solutions with words and pictures; and calculators and other classroom tools became part of the assessment process. Teachers began to ask important questions about how to align assessment practices with classroom instruction.

Some of those questions pertain to the use of manipulative materials. Pattern blocks, tangrams, Cuisenaire Rods, and base 10 blocks are a small sampling of the many materials used to teach and learn mathematics in today's K–12 classrooms. The use of such materials in the mathematics classroom has provided children with new ways to understand important concepts. The visual and tactile nature of such materials invites exploration by learners of all ages; the materials provide ways for students at all levels of mathematical development to make mathematical connections and to emphasize relationships among the quantities represented by the materials. In addition, these classroom tools naturally become part of the informal observations that teachers make while their students are engaged in group problem solving. However, what about more formal assessments? An important next step for teachers is to construct test questions that utilize different manipulative materials to assess the depth of their students' mathematical knowledge and understanding in authentic ways.

Why should mathematics teachers make the added effort to include manipulative-based questions or problems on a test? There are several important reasons. In mathematics classrooms where manipulative materials have been an integral part of learning, these hands-on questions help to align the assessments with the instructional process. Using the manipulative materials on the test also emphasizes to these learners that such activities are valued by their instructor. For students who have not completely mastered a particular concept, using hands-on questions honors their learning process and provides them with an opportunity to demonstrate their developing knowledge. Their open-ended responses help both the teacher and the learner to monitor progress in moving from a concrete understanding that is dependent on the materials to one that is more abstract and formalized.

The following discussion of hands-on assessment questions will give the reader an opportunity to observe how mathematical understanding can be measured through the use of specific manipulative materials. The course setting is a content course for pre-service elementary teachers, most of them enrolled in their first mathematics class since high school. Some of the questions are open-ended; others have a single correct answer. Some might also be classified as performance tasks where all students are expected to apply their conceptual knowledge in a new way (Danielson, 1997). Actual test questions and the students' responses to them are drawn from different areas of the mathematics curriculum.

Test Questions and Discussion

Numeration topics lay the basic foundation on which mathematical conceptual knowledge is constructed and developed. Within the K–8 curriculum, young students are expected to achieve proficiency in performing the four operations with whole numbers. As they progress through elementary school into middle school, their computational understandings must be extended to include fractions and decimal fractions. The K–8 students must develop a fundamental understanding of the meanings that are attached to the numeric values used as numerators and denominators in the written symbolism for fractions. The college students who are preparing themselves to teach mathematics in the elementary classroom must strengthen their own knowledge and understanding of fractions as well.

As part of classroom exploration, pre-service teachers were asked to attach fractional names to a wide variety of manipulative materials, including pattern blocks, Cuisenaire Rods, folded paper, and sections of circles. When asked to use the tangram pieces to illustrate one-half relationships, these students were able to show the fractional comparisons found in Figure 13.1. It is easily seen by area comparison that one of the small triangle pieces is half of the square piece, half of the parallelogram piece, and also half of the medium triangle.

Similarly, four of the small triangles will cover the large triangle, providing an illustration of the fractional value one-fourth. Two of the small triangles cover exactly one-

Figure 13.1 Tangram Pieces Illustrating One-Half Relationships

half of the large triangle, showing ¾ = ½. Classroom exploration time with tangrams and other materials allowed the pre-service teachers to explore three important conceptual ideas about fractions: 1) how the nature of one whole can change from one material to another, from one shape to another, or from one context to another; 2) how the concept of the denominator is connected to the number of same-size pieces needed to cover the whole; and 3) that fraction values may be named in equivalent ways.

The following assessment items show the degree to which students have internalized the concept of fraction representation using different manipulative materials that make use of an area model for fractions.

> **Example A.** *Some of the tangram pieces form a shape as shown. Find the correct fractional value for each piece if the area of the entire shape equals one whole.*

The student's work shown in Figure 13.2 demonstrates that she understands the concept of the unit fraction. Because 14 copies of the smallest triangle piece will cover the whole, she has named the small triangle to be ¹⁄₁₄ and

Figure 13.2 Example A

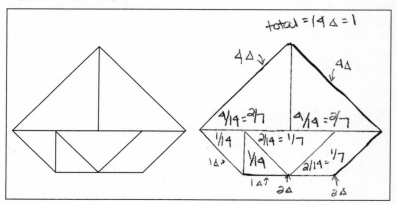

then correctly named the other pieces by comparing each area to that of the smallest triangle.

Pattern blocks are another common classroom manipulative. They are comprised of brightly colored flat blocks that fit alongside one another to make colorful patterns or designs. The individual pieces are yellow hexagons, red trapezoids, blue and white rhombi in two different shapes, green equilateral triangles, and orange squares. Their area relationships allow for fraction comparisons that extend their usefulness beyond building simple visual designs. The next assessment item provides a more open-ended way to assess the college students' understanding of fractional relationships.

> **Example B.** Use at least three colors of pattern blocks to cover one of the given shapes. 1) Trace the pieces to record how you covered the shape. 2) If the entire shape is considered to be one whole, briefly explain what fraction of the whole is covered by each color you used.

The outlined shapes in Figure 13.3 were deliberately selected for their reliance on fractions beyond the common values. The first can be covered by 16 small green triangles while

Figure 13.3 Example B

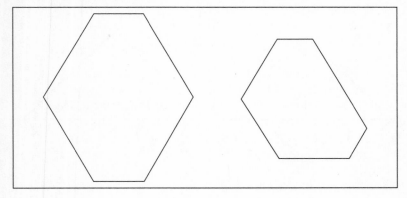

the second requires 14 small green triangles. Both diagrams require students to understand how the denominator value indicates the number of same-sized pieces required to cover the whole. To correctly complete the task, college students must understand this idea of covering the whole as well as the notion of equivalence.

Introductory work with the blocks allows students of all ages to easily see that one yellow hexagon is covered by two red trapezoids, or three blue rhombi, or six small green triangular pieces. In other words, the blocks lend themselves easily to fractions like ½, ⅓, and ⅙. In answering the assessment item posed in Example B, the pre-service students must choose how to cover the shape and then connect that covering with appropriate fraction names. Each student is able to choose an arrangement that makes sense, and the different possible arrangements lend themselves to multiple correct answers. The shapes used in this question require that students assign the value of 1/16 or 1/14 to the green triangle. For those students who understand the fractional relationship, this task is not significantly more difficult than using more common fraction values.

The work by the student on the left in Figure 13.4 shows a definite connection between her diagram and the correct fraction values, while the work on the right demonstrates a more limited understanding and a need for more practice on such tasks. The student's work on the left shows that she is comfortable assigning the values for each color of block. She has correctly counted the 16 triangles to cover the whole, and her dotted lines suggest that she is comparing each of the other pattern block areas to that unit fraction value of 1/16.

The second student has shown numerically that ⅓ = 2/6, which is a routine simplification of equivalent fractions. Viewed alone, this equation might suggest that the student grasps the concept. Unfortunately, she does not realize the contradictions in her picture. The yellow hexagon block covers the same area as two red trapezoids, so they should have the same fractional value. Instead, she has labeled

Figure 13.4 Examples of Fraction Values

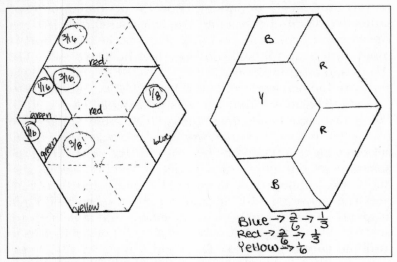

the blue and the red as equivalent values, possibly because there are two of each block. The student also does not seem to perceive that her total value should be one whole because she has a value of ⅙ unaccounted for in her calculations.

Simple paper folding can provide another means for practicing the concept of fraction representation. Again, there are many possible values beyond the common fractions, and students are pushed to consider equivalence and the interpretation of values that are not simple unit fractions.

Example C. A four-inch square of paper has been folded several times. The resulting fold lines are shown in the diagram. If the entire square represents 100%, label each area with an appropriate percent value.

The fractional concepts being assessed here are similar to those in the previous pattern block example. To correctly complete this task, college students must again consider the idea of covering the whole with a smallest piece to arrive at correct fraction values. The fraction values can then be converted to decimals. Observing their solution methods provides the instructor with information about the students' abilities to compare individual fractions with each other and with an appropriate unit fraction. The student work shown in Figure 13.5 demonstrates his competence with this task. He has determined that the smallest triangle is $\frac{1}{32}$ of the whole without needing to cover the entire square with small triangles. It is likely that he viewed the $\frac{1}{8}$ = 12.5% pieces first, seeing four rectangles in the upper half and four larger triangles in the lower half. He could then determine that the small triangle appears as $\frac{1}{4}$ of $\frac{1}{8}$ of the square, or $\frac{1}{32}$ of the whole square. He may have found the decimal for $\frac{1}{32}$ directly by calculating $1 \div 32 = 0.03125 = 3.125\%$, or he may have used the $\frac{1}{4}$ of $\frac{1}{8}$ relationship among the decimal values and correctly concluded that since $\frac{1}{8}$ = 0.125 = 12.5%, then the decimal for $\frac{1}{32}$ will similarly be $(0.125)/4 = 0.03125 = 3.125\%$. The four trapezoidal areas in the square are equivalent to $\frac{3}{32}$ or three copies of the smallest triangle. Those college students who recognize such multiples of the unit fractions and see that $\frac{3}{32} = 3(\frac{1}{32}) = 3(3.125\%) = 9.375\%$ have internalized a deeper understanding of proportionality and the relative size of the fractional pieces.

Figure 13.5 Example C

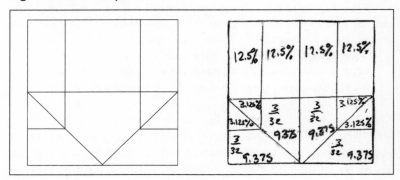

In addition to working on how numbers can be represented with fractional names, future teachers can deepen their numerical understanding by considering how numbers are represented in bases other than our familiar base 10. Commercial base 10 block sets consist of units (or ones), longs (or tens), flats (or hundreds), and a large cube (or thousands). These same sets are available in different base formats, such as base five or base six.

Using the materials in different bases is helpful in providing new insights about the four basic arithmetic operations. Most pre-service elementary students have used these operations accurately themselves, but few have considered the conceptual meanings of the operations. Materials in base six have helped college students focus directly on what it *means* to add, subtract, multiply, and divide numbers in this new base. Because the students can no longer rely on familiar algorithms and memorized number facts, the materials provide a structure for them to consider the physical actions associated with the four operations. Explaining the base six solution to the following division story problem demonstrates a deeper understanding of the operation itself.

> **Example D.** *Use your base six materials to demonstrate the step-by-step physical solution in base six to the story problem. Your answer should include diagrams and a written explanation of the physical process for finding the correct base six answer without any parallel conversion into base 10.* The primary classes at Euler's Elementary School are going to the Möbius Museum. Each school bus holds 102_{six} passengers plus a bus driver. How many buses are needed for the 340_{six} students plus 10_{six} adult chaperones?

The assessment objective for this problem is to determine whether students understand the meaning and process of the operation of division independent of our base 10 system. To successfully complete this task, students must have a working knowledge of place value groupings within the new base and an organizational system that will produce an accurate answer. After representing $340_{six} + 10_{six}$ with base six materials (three flats, five longs, and zero units), the students can repeatedly subtract off groups of size 102_{six} to represent each bus needed for the trip. The student work shown in Figures 13.6 and 13.7 demonstrates a comfortable understanding of both the operation and the base six numbers involved. Note that the students were working with base six materials they had previously constructed on their own—their sets consisted of wooden flats and longs with individual beans for the units.

Both college students approached the problem from a repeated subtraction understanding of division, separating

Figure 13.6 Example D (first student)

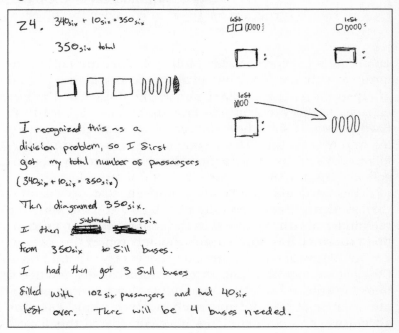

Figure 13.7 Example D (second student)

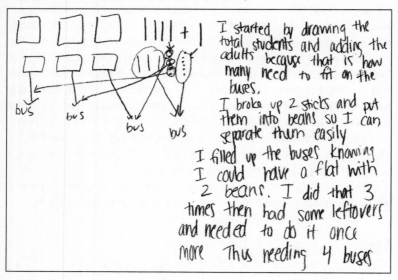

off portions to represent each full bus. They are both comfortable with the idea that division means making equal groups of a particular size, namely the divisor or the bus capacity in this problem. The first student (see Figure 13.6) used arrows to show how she rearranged the given materials into new groups. The second student (see Figure 13.7) followed a step-by-step method showing how many passengers are left after separating off each full bus.

This particular application problem also necessitates that students think carefully about how to deal with the remainder or leftover units. In the context of some application problems, it is appropriate to simply report the remainder. In this particular problem, it is necessary to round up to the next larger whole number of buses because a fractional bus does not make sense. Rounding down is inappropriate because some students or chaperones would miss the adventure, and both students have considered this aspect of the problem correctly.

The next curricular area to be considered is that of algebraic thinking or pattern finding. In the primary grades, the process may start with simple patterns like skip counting and gradually move toward writing functional rules as students learn to understand variables and the language of algebra. The following examples illustrate some manipulative approaches to helping future elementary teachers see and describe patterns in an algebraic manner.

> ***Example E.*** *Three steps of a growing tile pattern are shown* (Figure 13.8). *Choose one of the patterns shown; complete all three tasks for that pattern only. 1) Diagram the 50th arrangement of tiles in the sequence. Show the number of tiles that will be needed to build each linear section of the pattern. 2) Write the explicit general rule for the nth term in the sequence. 3) Use your rule to find the number of tiles needed to build the 305th arrangement of tiles.*

During class, groups of four students worked cooperatively with tiles on problems of this type. A fundamental goal of the activity was that students recognize growth pat-

Figure 13.8 Example E

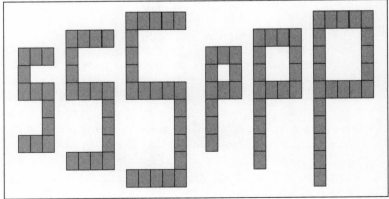

terns, to begin to write algebraic rules to describe the patterns, and to connect the symbolic rule to the changes that occurred with the tile arrangements themselves. On the S pattern, for example, each of the five linear segments grows by one tile each time. The number of tiles needed for each step comprise an arithmetic sequence (12, 17, 22, . . .) or a linear function given by the rule—Number of Tiles = 5n + 7—where n represents which step of the pattern is under consideration. As students think about connecting the physical model to the rule, they can relate the 5n (the changing or growing part) with the five linear tile sections that grow. In the third S, these five sections can be represented by the variable n as shown in Figure 13.9. The constant value of seven is directly linked to the corner and end point tiles with the seventh tile occurring in the vertical section that is one longer than the others. If students are able to make this physical correspondence between the rule and the equation, it represents a deeper

Figure 13.9 Sections Represented by the Variable *n*

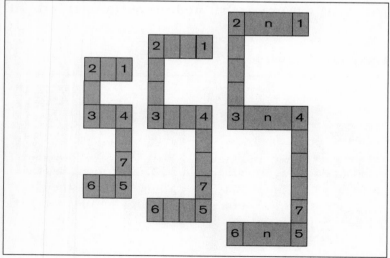

Figure 13.10 The Growing S Design

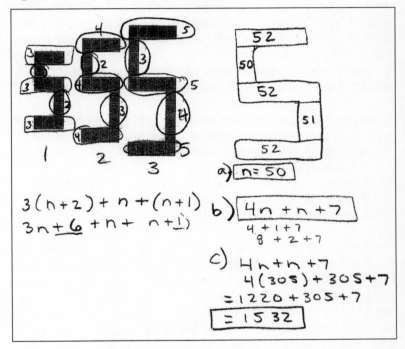

understanding of the mathematical concepts present in the problem. Asking students to graph the ordered pairs that relate term number to tile number (1,12), (2,17), (3,22) . . . might provide another window into their thinking about the concept of slope.

The circles drawn by the student in Figure 13.10 help me to assess her understanding of how the variable n is used in each step of the pattern. This student feels comfortable with the pattern, knows how to relate the change to the variable, and knows how to write the rule to describe further steps of the growing S design. She appears to have a substantive understanding of how a variable is used to connect this situation with the language of algebra.

Beyond numeration topics, a wide variety of manipulative materials and models have become a natural part of the geometry curriculum, helping students to visualize different two-dimensional shapes and three-dimensional solids. The following assessment question example pushes college students beyond the simple identification of shapes into establishing numerical relationships.

> **Example F.** *In a plastic tangram set, the smallest triangle has one right angle and its two shorter sides measure 3.5 cm each. Use that information and other relationships among the pieces to 1) mathematically establish the angle measurements of the parallelogram piece, and 2) calculate its side lengths (rounded to nearest tenth cm).*

The work shown in Figure 13.11 demonstrates how this future teacher is comfortable with the concepts present in this application. She sees how the parallelogram piece relates to the small triangles, and she applies the Pythagorean theorem correctly to find the missing side length. In addition, she is able to articulate and diagram her mathematical thinking in a very organized fashion.

The next geometry assessment task has many possible correct answers and it measures the depth of student understanding of the concept of symmetry. Recognizing that line or rotational symmetry exists is the first level of understanding followed by the ability to identify lines of symmetry and to classify rotational symmetry into broad groups. Creating an original design that displays symmetry of a particular degree measurement depends upon a deeper level of understanding, one that pays attention to how the structure of the underlying geometric shape will ultimately determine both the symmetry lines or the particular degree measurements of the final rotational symmetry that is present in the design.

Figure 13.11 Example F

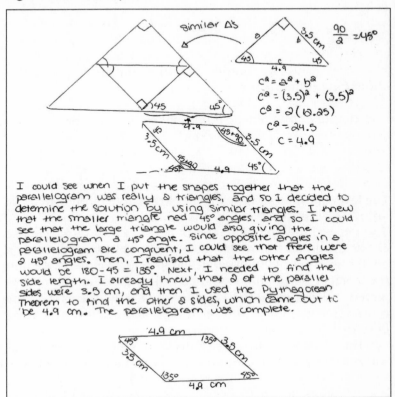

I could see when I put the shapes together that the parallelogram was really 2 triangles, and so I decided to determine the solution by using similar triangles. I knew that the smaller triangle had 45° angles, and so I could see that the large triangle would also, giving the parallelogram a 45° angle. Since opposite angles in a parallelogram are congruent, I could see that there were 2 45° angles. Then, I realized that the other angles would be 180 - 45 = 135°. Next, I needed to find the side length. I already knew that 2 of the parallel sides were 3.5 cm, and then I used the Pythagorean Theorem to find the other 2 sides, which came out to be 4.9 cm. The parallelogram was complete.

Example G. *On a separate sheet of paper, make a "connected" pattern block design that meets all of the following specifications: You must use a minimum of 12 blocks and at least 3 different colors of blocks. Your blocks should be "connected" along full edges. Your design should demonstrate rotational symmetry of 120°, 240°, and 360°. Your design should not display any visible line symmetry. Trace your final design and label the block colors.*

Figure 13.12 Example G

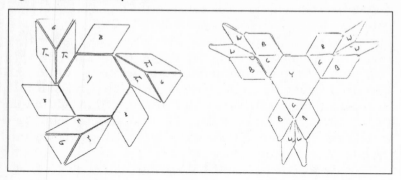

The level of understanding is quickly visible by the choice of an underlying structure by the individual college students. To successfully complete the task, students must choose either the green triangular piece or the yellow hexagon as a center starting piece. Both designs in Figure 13.12 exhibit the correct rotational symmetry; the student who completed the design on the right was not able to separate the rotational symmetry, and his design also shows three lines of reflection.

The work in Figure 13.13 displays rotational symmetry without line symmetry, but the degree measurements of 180°

Example 13.13 Rotational Symmetry Without Line Symmetry

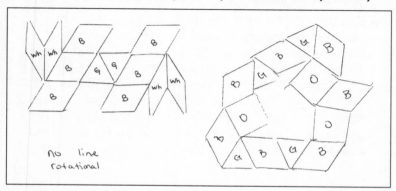

and 360° do not match with those assigned in the task. The student at the right was frustrated by the task and unable to construct the desired design. Her failure to use a center starting block demonstrates her limited understanding of how rotational symmetry is related to the center of any design.

Some tasks with manipulative materials can often be effective in pushing students to connect different concepts in the mathematical curriculum in a way that addresses higher order thinking skills. The next assessment item incorporates measurement, geometry, similar polygons, and proportionality within a single task. It was used after the college students had studied all of those curricular areas.

> **Example H.** Ask for a polygon piece. One of its edges is 3 centimeters long. Use appropriate tools to draw a precise enlargement of the piece on a separate page. In your enlargement, the 3-centimeter side should measure 5 centimeters.

Figure 13.14 Example H

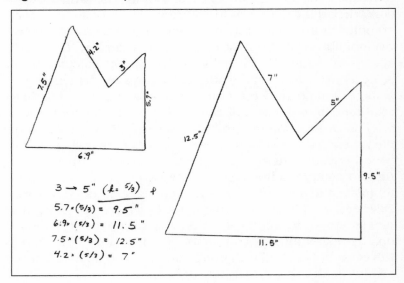

This problem provides an opportunity for students to synthesize several pieces of information in the completion of the assigned task. The direct measurement of individual side lengths is the most elementary of the required steps. To successfully complete the task, students must be comfortable with proportional reasoning and must understand the nature of similar figures. They must realize that enlarging by the scale factor of 5/3 will not change the overall shape of the original. This shape retention is an important characteristic of similar figures, one that occurs because the angle measurements do not change when all sides are increased proportionately. A simple metric ruler is the only tool required for this task. Students who understand the nature of proportionality and similar figures will realize that the angles can be copied directly from the pattern piece. When students request a tool such as a protractor for measuring angle sizes, it demonstrates to the instructor that their notions of similar figures are still being developed and refined.

Student work on this particular problem demonstrates different levels of student understanding. The student who constructed the diagrams in Figure 13.14 has a solid understanding of scale factor (denoted by $k = 5/3$) and also shows her comfort with both fractions and decimals. The work shown in Figure 13.15 includes her correct calculation of scale factor, but the use of different angle sizes demonstrates a more limited understanding of similar figures and their relationship to the task of enlarging a particular shape.

For this particular problem, several different problem pieces can be constructed, each with exactly one side of 3 centimeters in length. For evaluation purposes, the instructor can make "grading guides" by enlarging each piece for a template master to place over the top of each student's work. Discrepancies in the drawings quickly emerge to show any measurement inaccuracies and to reveal further the developing understanding of students who have not yet mastered the concepts of similar figures and proportional lengths.

Figure 13.15 Enlarging a Shape

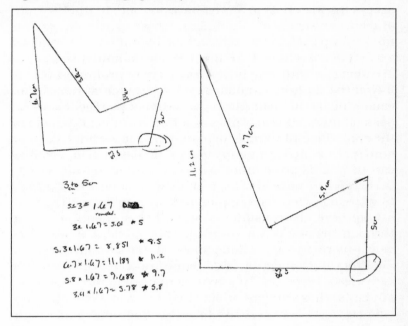

The sample assessment items discussed in this chapter have provided helpful information about the nature of individual student understanding. The use of the manipulative materials has allowed my college students to feel more comfortable in the testing situation; the familiar materials give them confidence to complete the assessment items to the best of their abilities.

Conclusion

As mathematics teachers at all levels begin to include such hands-on questions as part of assessments, there are logistical details to consider. The two most significant are the efficient distribution of materials and the appropriate time allowance. In a testing room, students need to be able to access the materials in a way that does not disrupt the work of fellow students. If all students possess personal collections of a particular material, the distribution is simplified and students simply take the needed manipulative materials along to the test. If not, then teachers must prepare individual bags or containers with enough materials for each student to complete a particular task. These may be passed out at the beginning of a test and then collected at the end. When the supply of materials is more limited, some students will need to complete a particular question so they can be passed on to other students. In that setting, it may be helpful to have the teacher move among the students to exchange or pass along materials. Another option is to set up several workstations and allow students to rotate through the stations as needed. This option may also provide a more private working space, if that is necessary.

Providing students with ample time to complete the activities is essential. This is particularly important for those students whose understanding may be incomplete on a specific concept. For students to feel comfortable exploring a new question through the materials, they must feel relaxed about the process. They will often work through a problem initially with only the materials and then go back to recheck their work and record their solution process afterward. Having ample time to complete these steps assures that the students have indeed been given an opportunity to demonstrate their understanding in the best possible manner.

Teachers may also want to construct a rubric to help standardize the grading of questions like those shown in this chapter. Because the questions may require more experienced students to explain thoroughly in writing how they used the materials, specific criteria to address writing quality should be considered. Sharing the rubric with the students prior to the testing situation will help them to feel comfortable with the manipulative tasks expected of them.

When the mathematics students are preparing to be teachers (like those students whose work is presented here), the inclusion of manipulative materials takes on a new significance. It helps these future teachers to develop a different mind set toward the materials, and more importantly, the subject of mathematics. Because their experiences with such materials are generally more positive than those with a more traditional symbolic or numerical approach, they are likely to carry their new enthusiasm for a hands-on approach to teaching, learning, and assessment into their own future classrooms.

The problems included in this chapter represent a starting point for the creation of other assessment questions that utilize a hands-on component. When students of all ages "think with their hands," they are able to demonstrate their understanding in different and authentic ways.

References

Danielson, C. (1997). *A collection of performance tasks and rubrics: Middle school mathematics.* Larchmont, NY: Eye on Education.

National Council of Teachers of Mathematics. (1989). *Curriculum and evaluation standards for school mathematics.* Reston, VA: Author.

14

Building Assignments Within Community: Assessment in the Real World

David B. Schock

Knowledge and time are really the only two gifts teachers bring to their students, and the ways teachers bring those gifts into their course design matters a good deal in the learning that's accomplished. In particular, I have found that two approaches make good use of the time I spend with students: service-learning and individualized learning.

No course I teach is purely theoretical: Every one puts students into the life of the community. Courses that have a component of outside involvement—service-learning—result in long-term learning. When students have to reach to meet not only an instructor's standards but also the expectations of an outside agent, suddenly the learning comes alive.

The second approach recognizes that education is an individual process; each student learns in his or her own way. That's why it's important for me to approach subjects with a respect for multiple learning styles and for individual differences. I design my courses so that *what* students learn reflects and builds on their interests and strengths. That means that I design assignments that ask students to make choices about what direction their learning will take and that allow their learning to be demonstrated in differing ways. Thinking of and relating to students as individuals (as opposed to the collective "class") presupposes one-on-one relationships between them and me. Approaching teaching in this manner is risky; it can be emotionally charged, but it is always personally rewarding.

In combination, these two elements—service-learning and individualized learning—deliver what students have consistently described in post-course evaluations as some of their most meaningful college experiences. This methodology has been discovered and described by many others, including the American Psychological Association (1997). Its web site (www.apa.org/ed/cpse/LCPP.pdf) reflects much of what I've found. Students learn by doing. In addition, students come to us with differing abilities and interests and differing ways of learning. Consequently, in assessing their learning, we need different kinds of measures. One test or one kind of test will not fit all students. If we want to know what they've learned, we need to take the time to seek the answers in several different ways.

What follows is a description of how I have put these fundamental principles into practice in an interdisciplinary course and in several communications courses.

First-Year Seminar

The first-year seminar (FYS) is a topical course whose purpose is to introduce beginning college students to college-level critical thinking and habits of mind. I decided to teach a course that explored juvenile delinquency and gangs in our area. The textbook was a challenging one for my 20, mostly white, mostly Midwestern students: *A Framework for Understanding Poverty* (2003) by Ruby Payne. It sets forth an understanding of what it means to be poor and to be locked in a social class. I called the course The Lost Children.

In addition to reading the text together, I wanted students to accomplish three goals: 1) to learn how to use Internet sources to gather more information about the topic; 2) to focus on some narrower aspect of the bigger problem (juvenile delinquency and gangs) and develop some expertise; and 3) to form a thesis for a 7- to 10-page essay on their topic. The students became responsible for teaching the class by collecting web sites related to juvenile delinquency and gangs, annotating them, and sharing them with the class.

Early on, students were trained to be discriminating about Internet sources. For example, they were urged to look at the currency of the information, the hosting sites and organizations, and the "About Us" sections. They also looked up information about authors. They learned to recognize and understand the nature of biases (not that those would necessarily make the students eschew the sites—but it was good for them to know). They learned about .org sites flying under false colors. If the site was deemed worthwhile, they were to name the subtopics to which it might be relevant, write an abstract, take note of any additional links the site provided, comment on the reliability of the data, and project the site's usefulness in their study of the larger topic: juvenile delinquency and gangs. Here's an example of a student's annotation of a web site:

Topics: Delinquency prevention, drug use prevention, mental health of youth, juvenile justice journals, victims of violent juvenile crime
Site address: http://ojjdp.ncjrs.org
Date: Updated in 2004
Host: Office of Juvenile Justice and Delinquency Prevention
Abstract: The OJJDP (Office of Juvenile Justice and Delinquency Prevention) is an organization set up to prevent juvenile delinquency. Their goal is to research the subject and continue to find as well as build delinquency-prevention solutions all over the United States.
Links: www.jrsainfo.org/jjec_(juvenile justice evaluation center); www.udetc.org (underage drinking enforcement center); www.foxvalleytech.com/ojjdp_ (missing and exploited children's training center)
Reliability (rating by reviewer): This web site is very reliable. There are many sources of information

found throughout the site. It has numerous links within the web site that provide articles, facts, and information about the organization and its research on the topic of juvenile delinquency.

Utility (rating by reviewer): I believe that this web site contains a lot of useful information. Being a national organization they have the ability to create a worthwhile web site that provides information as well as solutions to the juvenile delinquency problems of America.

Reviewed by: Jessica S. (The Lost Children)

Twenty students, each writing seven of these, created an active and useful database for research: 140 entries spread across the entire spectrum of online information about juvenile delinquency and gangs. The result was a research tool for everyone in the class to use for the next assignment: building a "text" that dealt with just one aspect of the topic that the student found interesting (e.g., gang initiation procedures, gang graffiti and tagging, unwed teen mothers, alternate high schools, or recidivism rates among juvenile offenders). The text was a printed version of 6 to 10 web sites related to a subtopic. The student's job was to find a focus, locate appropriate information, mark and annotate it, and compile it in a looseleaf binder. As a last step, students created their own "exam," an essay organized around a thesis about the subtopic that used the text they had created as a resource for data and interpretation. For example, if a student's interest was in gang initiations, he or she might write a final paper arguing that, no matter how much initiate suffered, admission to the gang family was worth the price. Because each student followed his or her own interests, there was slim likelihood that all students would share the same experience in the class; they would, after all, be creating different texts and writing about different topics related to the subject of lost children.

In addition to these activities, I wanted to bring meaningful events into the classroom and to move students out of the classroom. We started with a tour of the county's juvenile detention facility, one of the best in the nation. There, students not only looked into the pods, but they were also locked down. One very brave student volunteered to be strapped into the restraint chair. Students toured the classrooms, the gym, the adjacent courtroom where the juvenile cases are adjudicated, the showers, and the outside recreation area. They came back with their eyes opened; although all of them had gone to high school with students who'd been in a juvenile detention facility, not one of them had ever been inside such a place.

There were other events, too. Eighteen of the 20 students in the class signed up for an extra credit opportunity: some 20 hours of mentor training sponsored by Michigan State University, the land-grant college in our state. Mentor training, conducted by the county's extension agent for youth training, involves background checks for criminal behavior, suitability screening, and intensive training sessions that deal with effective ways to work with at-risk youth and their families. Students were instructed about policies and procedures; given an overview of the concepts and skills of mentoring, ways for setting appropriate boundaries, and understanding of youth development (physical, brain, emotional, and social development); and helped to develop effective communication skills (Michigan State University Extension, 2004). The college paid the modest cost (about $20 per student), and students finished as certified mentors qualified to start work in any number of youth-related activities such as the county Mentoring Collaborative, after-school programs, and Big Brothers Big Sisters. Many of them did become involved in these programs during the semester; some are still active at this writing.

Our in-class activities included relevant speakers. During one of the classes we hosted a local police officer who headed up the city's gang-related surveillance team. He brought along the former leader of the Latin Kings, a gang that has plagued our little town. This leader, Pedro, told of starting the gang and of the problems he now faces in his life as a result of his actions. My students had a chance to learn that gangs often are another kind of family, sometimes the only family a young person has. They also learned that leaders could come from anywhere. For his part, Pedro learned that his skills and experiences could translate to college admission after he finished his GED. Pedro, in fact, was so taken with the students and what they were doing with their lives that he kept conversations going with them and with me during the next two years.

Another guest speaker was a former student who had made a detour in her initial plans to pursue a career in business, deciding instead to spend her life working with kids in trouble. She had earned a master's degree in juvenile psychology and was now a school psychologist. Only a few years older than the students in the FYS course, she was a powerful role model and storyteller. She told us about the recent death of a former charge she had worked with at a nearby youth facility. She had remained friends with the girl after moving to her present job. In fact, she and her new husband had talked about adopting this child. The young girl was being transported from her youth home when she bolted from the van when it stopped; she was killed when she dodged into expressway traffic. There were tears in the classroom, and not all of them from my former student.

But we weren't done. There was enough time in the semester for me to approach the principal of the alternative education program in the public school district. She came into class with several of her students, and we held a wide-ranging conversation. My students and the high school students were roughly about the same age but from widely different backgrounds. From this initial contact, my students were invited to visit the alternative high school. We jumped on that in a New York minute, but I wanted to direct my students into an even deeper experience than just observing at the school. What could my students do that would give back?

It came to me that my students needed to sit down, one on one, and write what could be called social histories. So we needed to learn how to do that. We called on teachers of sociology and social work at both our college and the high school and we learned that social histories are dispassionate accounts of peoples' lives: descriptions of their families and home conditions. These social histories are used by schools and social service agencies to describe students and clients. A young woman might be the youngest child of four. Perhaps her mother has died or her father is incarcerated. There may be alcohol or other drug use by older siblings or aunts and uncles. There may be the stability of someone in the family who holds a job. The primary language may be Spanish or Laotian. The family might have a religious affiliation, and there may be family support for continuing education. My students learned to ask questions and then all they had to do was write up the account, preserving the anonymity of the high school student. I wasn't asking much.

Imagine my students, then, trudging through the early morning cold to go to a high school unlike any they'd ever known: a beat-up, worn-down building filled with young people who'd already fallen through the cracks in the system.

"Doc, I don't know what to tell them when they ask the name of our class."

"Give 'em the name: The Lost Children. Find out if that insults them or if it's inaccurate. That can be one of your questions."

A few minutes later: "Doc, they get it and they agree, but it sure feels funny to tell them about it. I was embarrassed."

That embarrassment didn't last long, and then my students were talking in some depth with the high school students. And things happened during the interview session! The high schoolers were delighted that somebody wanted to know about their lives. They poured out their hearts: stories of families in continual crisis, life as a 16-year-old single mother, incarceration at Juvie, drug abuse in the neighborhood and the home, violence, death, despair. But there were stories, too, of loving families, hope for the future, plans for more education, plans for work and families. And the high school students didn't stop with just talking about their own stories; they asked the college students about their lives, too. My pupils listened, wrote—carefully excising anything that could identify a specific student—and returned to share the products of their efforts. The alternative education students were amazed that somebody—anybody—cared enough about them to write down their stories. (Portions of one such social history are included in the appendix at the end of this chapter.)

I collected drafts of the social histories and then returned them for revisions. After the rewrite, students sent the work to the principal. She was doubly grateful to my students. She welcomed positive attention for her charges and published the stories of their social histories so community members (the board of education in particular) would better understand the pressures that confront students and teachers who operate at the edge of the system.

The high school students received copies of the stories and went so far as to have a celebratory breakfast on one of the last days of our semester. There we were in the cavernous gym of this ancient school. The hardwood floors under the drinking fountains were spongy with rot, and the paint had not been updated since the 1970s. The gym was clean and warm and that was about it. But something amazing happened: The breakfast and its conversation evolved into an impromptu talent show. I'm not sure who started the singing or which of my students demonstrated dance steps from a theater production she was involved with. I know that I heard Spanish and English, and I was amazed at the connections that were made.

What did my students learn? Certainly they practiced a series of conventional classroom skills: online research, the evaluation of Internet resources, organization, and written and oral communication. Each of these was relatively easy to assess because each was practiced in the public atmosphere of the classroom and its design. Everything they produced was intended not only for the teacher's eyes but also for the scrutiny of their peers and the outside people involved in the project. Beyond all of that, however, I was extremely happy with the less conventional skills and understandings my students learned and how they framed their learning as a new part of their lives. But just because I say my approach worked doesn't mean it's so. Were their lives really changed at the relational level, the level where we put learning into practice? There is some independent confirmation that such was the case. One of my colleagues in psychology conducted a survey of FYS classes at the start of the semester and at its conclusion to measure changes in racial attitudes of entering students. Of all the FYS sessions that dealt with topics that were culturally diverse, this course exhibited the second greatest change in participant attitudes. It was second only to the college's Phelps Scholars Program, a residential program that seeks out diverse students, encouraging "applications from African-Americans, Asian-Americans, European-Americans, Hispanic-Americans, and Native Americans, as well as international students from around the world" (Hope College, 2007). And it was a close second. The researcher, Mary Inman, put it this way: "Your students changed as much as the Phelps Scholars did!" (personal communication, July 21, 2005).

In a subsequent communication to those who encourage and administer the FYS session, she wrote this:

> Indeed, I'm finding most gains/enlargement in Phelps students, then in CD [culturally diverse] students, then in non-CD-FYS students. Interestingly, I found that David Schock's CD-FYS class was showing the

"most" enlargement of the CD-FYS classes. I have been talking to David to see what he did in class. He provided students with many experiential activities where his students were learning about poverty, racism, drugs, schooling with "lost children." Just thought I'd let you know that your moral and financial support to David and others for this "experiential learning that takes place outside [the school's] walls" seemed to enlarge students' definitions of racism to include "subtle" racism (same finding for white students in Phelps Scholars Program). (M. Inman, personal communication, July 22, 2005; Inman, 2005)

For this class of white middle- and upper-middle-class first-year students, taking the course meant encountering another reality, and that reality changed their perceptions of the world. Indeed, the nature of experiential learning is such that we usually *are* changed. I know I was.

Other Applications

This method has served my students well in other courses. And while it's true that applied courses might be more easily positioned to take advantage of the surrounding community, it is also true that opportunities to engage with the world outside the classroom are sometimes ignored. Here are some examples of how such engagement has worked in other, less likely courses.

Introduction to Mass Media

In this seven-week, half-term course, students learn to do social science research by designing and administering telephone and email surveys about media consumption in the college and local community. Students come up with the topics (e.g., the perceived trustworthiness of news media, the public's recall and response to Super Bowl commercials, the use and abuse of the Internet, or film rankings), many of them wonderfully creative. Faculty from the college's professional research office help students frame their survey questions. The most recent survey made use of peer-to-peer questioning, and one student had the bright idea to use Facebook to reach members of her high school graduating class. Other students did the same. Amazing . . . using a new communication technology for research! I *never* would have thought of this in a million years! And the return rate? Close to 70%. Seventy percent on a survey!

Media Production I

In this course, the final project involves students with local nonprofit service organizations like Big Brothers Big Sisters and United Way. After mastering the basics of audio and video technology, students find an organization that wants their help. They research its operations, the people served, the budgets and staffing assignments, the previous outreach and advertising campaigns, competitors' advertising, and whatever issues the organization faces. For example, a student might pick the Center for Women in Transition. After research, the student might learn that what's needed is a campaign about the nurse practitioner program; or the wardrobe program (business attire that's loaned out so women can be well dressed for job interviews); or the education program that deals with date rape, domestic violence, or homelessness prevention. In addition to a written report, the student crafts three radio ads and one television ad that the center will be able to use if it chooses. And the center *has* used student-produced work in the past.

This final and capstone project for the class does several things. First, the student is responsible for choosing the assignment and making all of the contacts. This drives students into the community and eliminates any perception that the college is hermetically sealed. Second, students realize that what they do matters, and not just in an academic way. This is more than a graded exercise that only the professor will see. In fact, because we use the television ads in our student-run news show, these ads will be shown in the larger community of 9,000 homes. Third, because production makes use of multiple talents, students are forced to rely on each other for help. Not all students will do everything well, and they are taught that while they can do almost anything in production, they won't be able to do it by themselves. So the student in charge may write and produce the commercial but will rely on others to help with lighting, audio, on-screen talent, videography, and editing. Students are challenged to solve practical problems ranging from shooting good video or still pictures to dealing with copyright issues for background music. In all of their work on this project, they are responsible not only to themselves and their professor, but also to an outside client.

Students often pull all-nighters in the edit suites and need extra help to remember editing basics and the application of advanced tricks. Students from former semesters who are still very much interested in the field often volunteer a couple of hours of assistance. In doing so, past and present students create their own learning community. And they know it works.

The formal assessment of the students' projects takes into account all of the parts: client contact (there's a reporting form for these clients), research, copywriting, production, and presentation. It's amazing to see where students develop strengths across this spectrum.

Media Production II

The budding broadcast journalists in my Media Production II class learn about libel, intrusion, FCC rules and regulations, tax bases, millages, cops, and courts, but they do so while they are preparing a program to go live on cable. Like music, the point of rehearsal is to perform. My students have one week of pure rehearsal, and then during the next 14 weeks they both rehearse and perform, live, twice a week for a half-hour broadcast. The product is our small city's only local television newscast. They learn a lot in a short time, and they understand it in a way that students who only practice cannot. Generally they start by covering events that are close to home on the campus. But with a little prodding they range further afield: city and county events, breaking news, and local issues. It often comes as a surprise to them when they are recognized in local stores, even when they go out for a cup of coffee. And they hear—sometimes very bluntly—what people think of their work. Most often they are thanked for doing something local.

About midterm in the semester—for various reasons, many to do with lack of sleep—these students slack off just a little. It is then that I tell them they are in competition for jobs, but they are not in competition with me or necessarily the other members of the class. Their competition is *anybody* who will be hitting the job market at the same time they will at graduation. I assure them that while they may do enough to earn a good grade in the class, it won't be enough to snag a job; that always takes effort above and beyond. One of their exercises is to shadow a professional who does a job they'd like to do—reporter, videographer, assignment editor, producer, news director, or anchor. I tell them their best shot to enter the field is as an assistant producer and that anchors must first have a lot of success as reporters. These visits serve as a wake-up call for the kinds of mastery required to enter the field. And the professionals—who are always very kind—are also dead-on about where the students stand in terms of being ready for more than a local show.

Media Production IV

In this documentary course my students have had the greatest opportunity to serve. We decided in the 2002 fall semester to do a documentary about a 25-year-old unsolved homicide. The victim was Janet Chandler, a former student who had studied at the college where I was teaching. Abducted from her night job at a local motel, her body was found the next day along a highway. The family welcomed our interest. My students' initial reaction was one of fearful attraction. They were roughly the age of Janet when she'd been murdered. "You're creeping me out, here, Doc," said one young woman when I proposed the idea. They needed time to think. So did I.

Over the course of a week we discussed the idea with each other and the students went so far as to talk with their families about it. We came together with a purpose and then we started to gather the story, researching, finding people to interview, and locating addresses where people lived. When it came time to interview Janet's parents and brother, one of my students came out to the car as I was readying equipment to go into the house. "I am so far out of my comfort zone," he said. I responded, "Me too. And if you weren't, I'd really be concerned about you. Now, let's get in there and do what we can. You'll find your feet; just pay attention." And I was able to assess that my students quickly displayed traits of compassion, gentleness, care, and empathy. I think that at some point all of us cried that day.

We came back to our house where my wife encouraged the students to sit and relax, and we ordered pizza. This was a chance to discuss what had transpired and their reactions. There was a whole lot of assessing going on. Their resolve was firm: We're telling this story. The resulting film was shown at the college-owned theater and then aired on an area public television affiliate. Out of the film came enough public discussion that police fielded an investigative team. After 18 months the police made their first arrest in the case. Five others followed shortly thereafter— all as a result of going where we feared to go. The experience created a bond among the students. In fact, seven of the eight students from that term returned to campus when NBC's *Dateline* came to share their part of the story. No matter what grade I gave them for the course, they have been assessed by a much larger community.

My documentarians and I have followed year by year with other cold cases. The police have gone from suspecting our motives to asking for our help. The assessment of the community is clear: We're doing something that matters to other people.

And that's it, really, doing something that matters: teaching. Helping students to do things that will change their lives. Walking with them through experiences that leave us all changed.

Conclusion

I want my students involved with more than the world of the classroom. That's why assignments are framed in the context of a much larger scope, trying to look with new eyes, trying to think of ways that any assignment could have a larger impact. And the relationships among us—as teacher and students, within the community of the college, and within the community at large—might result in lasting bonds.

There are risks, to be sure. Some things flat out failed. But the risks—when carefully considered—are well worth it. I wouldn't have missed this for the world, and the relationships we've created are rich beyond price.

Appendix

Excerpts from Janelle's Story— Quiet Heartbreak

By Rachel

She's a petite 15-year-old with blonde hair, a dimpled chin, and almond blue eyes. In many respects she is an average teenager. Janelle likes to shop for clothes, makeup, and shoes, play pool, hang out with friends at the mall or at her home, read Stephen King, and watch TV. As is the case for most busy teenagers, her perfect day would consist entirely of sleep. Janelle has never been abused or neglected; in fact, nothing arguably traumatic has ever happened to her. But despite its lack of sensational events, her life has been filled with heartbreak.

Q. What was your childhood like?
A. Rough.
Janelle grew up in a small town about a 45-minute drive from Benton Harbor, Michigan. Currently she lives with her family in Holland, Michigan. Her dad was a mechanic who was frequently paid in drugs. As a small child, Janelle remembers going to work with her dad then being left alone for 15 minutes at a time while her dad and his friends used and traded drugs in the shop bathroom.

Her dad was also physically abusive. Although he never touched her, he abused her older brothers and her mom. Whenever her mom would summon the courage to report her husband's behavior to the police, Janelle's dad would serve jail time. But on his release, Janelle's mom would always let him return. She insisted that she "loved him" and she reasoned that her children needed a father.

Q. Are your basic needs met?
A. No.
Janelle now lives with her mom and one of her two older brothers, age 23. Janelle mourns the absence of a father figure. Her brother attempts to play that role, but in her own words, "It doesn't work too well." They argue frequently.

Q. What's the nicest thing anyone has done for you?
A. Little things. Rides home, favors, attention.
Janelle seems to be a person who is starved for attention, especially from adults. She relates that her favorite part of school is talking with the teachers. She recently began dating another student at Holland Alternative High School, a friendly 17-year-old with a beautiful smile. The other quality that attracted her to him was the respect with which he treated her. The crude sexual jokes that she receives on a daily basis from other boys have never come from him.

Janelle's most prized possession is the last letter she received from her grandpa before he passed away last year. "Well, he was not really my grandpa," she amends. He was a family friend who supported her throughout her childhood in the absence of her dad. He even gave her family rent-free housing.

Q. Do you feel you are a successful person?
A. No. I don't have nothing to be successful about.
Janelle first began attending Holland Alternative High School in the middle of her first semester of ninth grade. She was making poor grades and even felt physically unsafe at her public high school. Janelle has been on probation for three years. She describes herself as having an "attitude and anger problem." She sometimes explodes when she gets angry, rebelling against any teachers who try to reason with her. This has caused her major trouble.

Not surprisingly, Janelle defines success as having a high school diploma, a college degree, and a good job. She claims not to know many successful people because her acquaintances have no diplomas and work low-paying jobs at fast food restaurants and gas stations. But she thinks that with time, she will become a successful individual.

Q. Do you have any advice for preteens?
A. It's hard to be a teenager. There's going to be problems—just be strong and live through it.

After I talked with Janelle the first two times, I had a very positive feeling that her story would have a happy ending. She has diagnosed her attitude problem, which is the first step to dealing with her issues. She has a supportive mom and she has dreams and ambitions. But my naive optimism was shattered when I returned to her school a third time to meet with her and found that she had been suspended for five days.

At first her behavior seemed incomprehensible. How could a girl with so much potential continue to get herself in so much trouble?

I suppose that I shouldn't have been surprised. Human beings continue to make mistakes all the time, even when they are perfectly aware that they need to change. I have done the same thing myself more times than I like to remember. And as much as I would like to end her story with a bright word of encouragement, I know that it would not be realistic. Janelle has had a difficult life for one so young. I can only hope that she will choose to climb back onto the path to success and create her own "happily ever after" ending.

References

American Psychological Association. (1997). *Learner-centered psychological principles: A framework for school redesign and reform.* Washington, DC: Author.

Hope College. (2007). *Frequently asked questions.* Retrieved May 9, 2007, from the Hope College, Phelps Scholars Program web site: www.hope.edu/phelps/faq.htm

Inman, M. (2005). *Enlarging definitions of racism with cultural diversity: Classes and college symposium.* Unpublished manuscript.

Michigan State University Extension. (2004). *Mentor manual.* East Lansing, MI: Author.

Payne, R. K. (2003). *A framework for understanding poverty* (3rd rev. ed.). Highlands, TX: aha! Process, Inc.

Conclusion: Do Classroom Assessment Techniques Improve Student Learning and Fulfill Larger Assessment Goals?

Scott VanderStoep, Carla Reyes

In this concluding chapter we explore two issues related to assessment of student learning. The first is the impact of classroom assessment procedures at the micro-level, specifically the effects on student learning. We approach this analysis from the perspective of self-regulated learning theory. Specifically, we examine how classroom assessments might positively or negatively affect student learning and motivation. The second issue is the impact of classroom assessment procedures at the macro-level, specifically the effects on curricular changes, campus assessment programs, and institutional decision-making. For the second issue we examine the important topics—the emphasis on standards, feedback loop, and faculty participation—that currently occupy a large part of the assessment dialog that takes place on campuses.

Micro-Level Concerns: Classroom Assessment and Student Learning

A Theoretical Framework for Understanding Student Learning and Motivation

This discussion will frame the issue of classroom assessment techniques from the perspective of a researcher interested in student learning and motivation. Most psychologists who study student learning approach it from the perspective of self-regulation. A self-regulated learner is one who actively plans, monitors, and controls his or her own learning behavior (VanderStoep & Pintrich, 2007) and who uses effective cognitive strategies such as elaboration and organization, effective metacognitive strategies such as planning and goal setting, and has more adaptive motivation beliefs such as high self-efficacy, interest in the course topic, and task persistence. The first wave of research on self-regulated learning showed that students who adopted a mastery goal orientation—a focus on learning and mastery of the content—exhibited more adaptive outcomes such as those just described (e.g., Dweck & Leggett, 1988). In contrast, students who adopt a performance goal orientation—a focus on ability and performance outcomes—show greater concern with how their performance compares to others, not wanting to appear incompetent, and avoiding tasks that may result in "failure" (Pintrich, 2000b). The educational advantage thought to be the purview of a mastery orientation has come to be known as normative goal theory.

More recently, however, revised goal theory has found that sometimes a performance goal orientation may be adaptive (Middleton & Midgley, 1997; Pintrich, 2000a). Specifically, students who focus on approach performance goals have more adaptive learning strategies and successful outcomes than those who focus on avoidance performance goals. An example of an approach performance goal would be trying to outperform others or to demonstrate one's ability or competence to others, such as receiving a scholarship or departmental award. An example of an avoidance performance goal would be engaging in learning behaviors that help a person avoid looking incompetent, such as setting a goal that is so impossibly high to achieve that the difficulty serves as a built-in excuse for failure. From this revised goal theory perspective, performance goals may not always be bad.

In the first section of this chapter, we examine the role of assessment in higher education from the perspectives of goal theory and self-regulation. The objective is to assist those interested in developing classroom assessment to understand the effects that such assessments might have on students' self-regulation and goal orientation.

In general, assessment techniques that promote either a mastery orientation or an approach performance orientation will have a positive impact on student learning. We see many examples of how the assessment tools described in this book will facilitate adaptive learning and goal setting on the part of the students—either a mastery orientation or an approach performance orientation. We will mention these particular techniques where relevant.

Classroom Assessment and Student Functioning

We now examine more closely the specific constructs from self-regulation theory that are related to classroom assessment techniques (Angelo & Cross, 1993). Although there are various components of self-regulation theory that we could cover, we focus our discussion on two aspects that we believe are most potentially impacted by classroom assessment techniques. Specifically, we explore the impact of classroom assessment on students' motivational beliefs and on students' cognitive strategies.

Classroom assessment and motivational beliefs. Three of the motivational beliefs that are studied frequently by educational psychologists are self-efficacy, task value, and test anxiety. Self-efficacy is the extent to which one feels competent and confident in a particular area of study or performance. This is differentiated from self-esteem, which is understood to be a more global measure of self-worth (VanderStoep & Pintrich, 2007). Research has shown that self-efficacy is tied to attributions about success and failure—the self-generated reasons for success or failure on a particular academic task (e.g., classroom assessment). Specifically, students' self-efficacy will be affected by the location of the attribution (internal to the person vs. part of the external environment); the stability of the attribution (situation staying the same vs. situation changing); and the controllability of the attribution (student can control this aspect of their learning vs. they cannot). For example, if students believe that success comes from hard work, then this would be an internal attribution; if students believe that they failed because they were stupid, then this would be a stable attribution; if students believe that with extra effort and instructional enrichment they can improve, then this would be a controllable attribution. Educational psychologists are most interested in students' response to failure on assessment techniques, and it has been shown that the most adaptive attributional pattern in response to failure is for students to make an attribution that is external ("I was too busy this week and didn't have time to study"), unstable ("It won't happen again"), and controllable ("Next time I'll plan ahead better so I don't have to cram"). This is far better than students making internal, stable, and uncontrollable attributions. ("I'm not good at history, I'll never be good at history, and there's nothing I can do about it.") The former attributional pattern will help to buoy self-efficacy even in the face of difficulty or failure on an assessment, whereas the latter will produce lower self-efficacy.

Although the theory and research in the area are quite robust, we recognize that these cognitions are probably running in the subconscious background of students' minds most of the time. We also recognize that even psychologists who understand this research do not construct assessment instruments with students' self-efficacy beliefs as a top concern. Still, it is important to understand that during classroom assessments, especially important or high-stakes assessments, that students' self-beliefs are more salient to them than perhaps we as faculty members recognize. Furthermore, when students receive assessment feedback, they are very self-focused. This heightened sense of self-awareness may exacerbate self-efficacy cognitions.

The concept mapping technique presented by Richard J. Mezeske (Chapter 2) may be helpful with respect to self-efficacy because it leaves space for students to demonstrate what they know, rather than highlight what they don't know.

The grading procedure outlined by Thomas Smith (Chapter 6) that allows students to provide justification for their answers may send the message to students that performance and ability are not stable and uncontrollable, but rather are changeable with student effort. This technique may therefore produce more adaptive attributional patterns.

Task value refers to the extent to which activities are seen as useful, worthwhile, and relevant. Classroom assessment techniques that are void of context would likely lower students' perceptions of task value. We encourage faculty to wed their assessment techniques as much as possible to phenomena that would be a part of the professional life of someone studying in this field. This book is replete with such activities, and we recommend these ideas to others in the respective fields. We mention several here with the understanding that all of the chapters do well to promote a sense of task value. Lee Forester's (Chapter 7) emphasis on engaging students in German culture brings to life the important aspects of living in Germany. Michael Misovich and Roger Veldman's (Chapter 10) assessment technique emphasizes team projects like those found in industry. Kathy Winnett-Murray's (Chapter 5) revival of the lab practical teaches students basic lab skills that they will use after graduation. And Janis M. Gibbs's (Chapter 4) historiography assignment puts students in the role of historian in a very authentic way.

Finally, test anxiety is perhaps the most relevant motivational construct when it comes to classroom assessment techniques. Educational psychologists usually break test anxiety into two parts: emotionality—heightened physiological arousal that results in decreased performance—and cognitive interference—the stress of assessment lowers one's ability to think well (VanderStoep & Pintrich, 2007). It is widely understood that students with little or no test anxiety do not take the assessment seriously enough and will not perform up to their potential. Conversely, students with anxiety that is too high will produce the negative consequences of emotionality and cognitive interference. It is usually recommended that faculty create a moderate amount of anxiety with their assessment techniques—enough to make students work hard and take the assessment seriously but not so high that students are emotionally overwhelmed and do not function up to their potential. We recognize that there is no measure of test anxiety that will indicate to a professor that he or she has developed a technique that has the appropriate amount of anxiety. We also recognize that individual differences in anxiety make it even more difficult to produce a classroom assessment technique that is at the moderate level for all students. However, instructors bring with them experiences about what produces anxiety in students based on previous use of classroom assessments. We were intrigued by Thomas Smith's approach to grading the exam with the student present. At first glance, this would seem to produce a great deal of test anxiety. (We usually think of anxiety occurring during the exam, but this would actually happen after the exam.) But as he describes it, such is not the case. It would be interesting to collect data on student anxiety in his class compared to a similar class taught without this particular assessment technique.

Classroom assessment and students' cognitive strategies. Our discussion of learning strategies will focus on two broad categories: 1) cognitive learning strategies such as rehearsal, elaboration, and mental organization, and 2) metacognitive learning strategies such as planning, goal setting, and self-monitoring.

With respect to cognitive strategies, self-regulated learners are those who match their strategies with the needs of the assessment technique. If an assessment technique is strictly a multiple-choice exam of the definitions from the lecture notes, then students are likely to engage in a large amount of rote rehearsal of the notes with little or no emphasis on careful textbook reading or higher level learning strategies. In other words, if low-level rehearsal of definitions is sufficient to succeed on the classroom assessment, then that is likely what students will do. A fairly robust finding in research on student learning is that when students engage in higher level learning strategies, such as elaboration and mental organization, the result is a deeper and more complex understanding of the material. To that end, classroom assessment techniques that require students to engage in these higher-level strategies will produce better cognitive outcomes. This book has many examples of classroom assessment techniques that do just that. Richard J. Mezeske's concept mapping idea is an important technique that helps students build rich cognitive structures. Such a classroom assessment technique is widely understood to produce high-level learning (McKeachie & Svinicki, 2006). Mary DeYoung's (Chapter 13) assessment of pre-service teachers' knowledge of mathematics requires a higher level of thinking than traditional problem-solving assessment. And Thomas Smith's requirement that students explain their answers during the grade-with-professor session is a great way to determine if students have a more complex understanding than what can otherwise be demonstrated on a normal classroom exam. In general, these assessment techniques do well in facilitating higher level cognitive strategies.

With respect to metacognitive strategies, self-regulated learners are those who show higher levels of planning, goal setting, and self-monitoring. The most effective classroom assessment techniques will prompt students to engage in higher levels of self-monitoring. Specifically, such techniques cause students to reflect on what they know, recognize what they don't know, and identify ways to change their study habits so they can improve their understanding. Thomas Smith's approach to grading the exam while the student is present *forces* the student to be self-aware. Perhaps a "how to improve" session at the end of the grading period might help students with planning for future exams. However, given the high labor costs already involved in such an ambitious endeavor, we are hesitant to recommend changes that increase the workload. Such a technique already does much to promote students' self-monitoring of learning. Susan Cherup's (Chapter 9) approach also has the capacity to promote self-monitoring. This is done in a very direct way—by asking students to evaluate their performance at their field placement and self-assess their presentation skills. Self-assessment cannot be done in isolation or even count as a majority of one's evaluation. However, self-assessment, if done with integrity, can promote students' metacognitive strategy use.

Macro-Level Concerns: Classroom Assessment and Campus-Wide Assessment

In this final section we move from a concern over how classroom assessment techniques impact student learning to how classroom assessment techniques impact campus-wide assessment concerns. We do this by describing three major concerns that we believe are at the forefront of campus discussion about assessment: 1) developing and maintaining standards, 2) using classroom assessment to inform curricular, pedagogical, and institutional concerns, and 3) getting faculty to buy in to the assessment enterprise.

Standards

Many believe that assessment in higher education is driven by external forces. At the department level, areas of study that have national accrediting organizations are usually the departments on campus that have the best assessment plans in place. In undergraduate institutions these are often teacher education, nursing and other allied health fields, dance, and engineering. At the graduate level, a program such as clinical psychology that seeks accreditation of its program and licensure of its graduates would also have strong assessment plans.

One common feature of such accredited programs is the presence of standards. Departments are required to demonstrate that a certain percentage of their students are performing at or above a level identified by the accrediting agency. If standards fall below a specified level, the program's accreditation goes on probation or is suspended.

As excited as we are about the authentic and forward-looking classroom assessment techniques described in this book, in some ways we wonder whether techniques like these move departments closer to or away from developing standards. Covington (1992) would argue that educational bureaucrats and politicians have confused standards with standardization—they are not the same thing. One can have high standards without having standardized assessment instruments. Covington's point is well taken, and this book highlights that one can hold students to a high standard without conforming to a standardized approach to assessment. However, many faculty still feel the push toward standardized assessment amidst the current version of the so-called accountability movement. (As a case in point, the day this chapter was being written, the U.S. Department of Education released its report on accountability in higher education. Part of this report addressed moving toward developing a national student database. Although not directly related to the issue of standardized tests, it is clear that the federal government is moving toward standardization of data in higher education.)

We largely agree with Covington that programs can be rigorous in the absence of standardized assessments. But we also see the virtue in providing some standardized assessment instrument. The standardized instrument need not appear at the course level but perhaps at the department level. The following anecdote may serve as an illustration to which many can relate. Recently a department chair was discussing academic rigor in his department with his divisional dean. The topic of assessment of student learning quickly arose during the conversation. The dean was concerned that, on paper, this particular department did not have nearly as many required courses or credit hours as other departments. The dean questioned how this department can have high standards with nearly (in some cases) 12 credit hours fewer than other departments. One way to address this issue is through standardization. Thus, the issue was resolved by agreeing to have that department conduct a standardized assessment of its graduating seniors. If the seniors in this program perform at a high level on a nationally normed achievement test, then concern over rigor or depth of coverage becomes less so. But if graduates perform poorly on a standardized test, it may suggest an urgent need to make some curricular changes including increasing the number of credits required for a major.

This kind of standardized assessment, we contend, must also move forward. Department chairs and administrators must find ways to encourage the new and exciting types of classroom assessments found in this book while still being aware of national trends in assessment that are moving toward standardization.

Feedback Loop

A vital component to a healthy assessment program is a mechanism by which the data get plugged back into the course, department, division, or institution. The often-called "feedback loop" allows educators to determine if their pedagogical goals are being achieved. Evidence that the feedback loop is in place comes in the form of pedagogical, curricular, or college-level changes that are implemented based on the data. Most assessment professionals and site visitors look for the presence of this feedback mechanism as evidence of a mature assessment plan.

Janis M. Gibbs's chapter on assessment in European history mentions her department's need to teach students how to write a research paper prior to the capstone course. This is an example of a classroom assessment technique flowing from departmental goals. Similarly, Rhoda Janzen (Chapter 12) notes that her department received troubling feedback about the ability of its students to teach grammar and even the students' knowledge of grammar. Richard

Ray's (Chapter 11) documentation and analysis of clinical transcripts is a thorough way to ensure both that nothing falls through the cracks in the major and to give future employers feedback about specific strengths and weaknesses of the department's graduates. As he notes, it also provides faculty with information about which skills take the most time to learn, which skills are the easiest to learn, and the relationship between clinical performance and other achievement measures.

Effective classroom assessment techniques in the absence of departmental goals and feedback become little more than "gee whiz" activities that students enjoy. We encourage all faculty who are interested in developing creative assessments to keep in mind the larger purpose of the endeavor as they design such creative techniques as those described in this book.

Faculty Participation

It is difficult to go to an assessment conference and not hear assessment coordinators speaking unhappily about how difficult it is to get faculty to buy in to the assessment enterprise. Perhaps the most inspirational part of reading this book is the fact that all of these creative assessment techniques were created by the very faculty that the assessment directors need to buy in. In addition, all of these faculty members have generated these creative assessment techniques on their own. Too often it is said that assessment is top-down, accreditation-driven, or in some other way heavy-handed, rather than originated by professors working in the trenches. Such is not the case with these techniques. They were derived from faculty recognizing a need in their course or department and implementing a plan to collect important data on student learning—this is the essence of effective assessment. If for no other reason, this set of creative classroom assessments will serve faculty well as they seek to engage and challenge their students; they will serve assessment directors who are constantly searching for examples of how classroom assessment can be done seamlessly and without appearing heavy-handed; and they will serve institutions of higher learning as they face mounting pressures from governmental and accrediting institutions for accountability.

References

Angelo, T. A., & Cross, K. P. (1993). *Classroom assessment techniques: A handbook for college teachers* (2nd ed.). San Francisco, CA: Jossey-Bass.

Covington, M. V. (1992). *Making the grade: A self-worth perspective on motivation and school reform.* New York, NY: Cambridge University Press.

Dweck, C. S., & Leggett, E. L. (1988). A social-cognitive approach to motivation and personality. *Psychological Review, 95*(2), 256–273.

McKeachie, W. J., & Svinicki, M. (2006). *McKeachie's teaching tips: Strategies, research, and theory for college and university teachers* (12th ed.). New York, NY: Houghton Mifflin.

Middleton, M. J., & Midgley, C. (1997, December). Avoiding the demonstration of lack of ability: An underexplored aspect of goal theory. *Journal of Educational Psychology, 89*(4), 710–718.

Pintrich, P. R. (2000a). Multiple goals and multiple pathways: The role of goal orientation in learning and achievement. *Journal of Educational Psychology, 92*(3), 544–555.

Pintrich, P. R. (2000b). The role of goal orientation in self-regulated learning. In M. Boekaerts, P. R. Pintrich, & M. Zeidner (Eds.), *Handbook of self-regulation* (pp. 451–502). San Diego, CA: Academic Press.

VanderStoep, S. W., & Pintrich, P. R. (2007). *Learning to learn: The skill and will of college success* (2nd ed.). Upper Saddle River, NJ: Prentice Hall.

Index